Brute Force

Brute Force

◆ ◆ ◆

Animal Police and the Challenge of Cruelty

Arnold Arluke

Purdue University Press ◆ West Lafayette, Indiana

Printed in the United States of America

Grateful acknowledgment is made to the following photographers for the use of images in this book:

Candace Cochrane: "Seized cat in cage," p. 127; "Dog tied up," p. 13
Dianne DeLucia: author photo, dust jacket
Patrice Flesch: "Beautiful Joe and Officer," p. 148
Michelle Segall/*Morning Union* (Springfield Newspapers): "Ox-pull inspection," p.146

Library of Congress Cataloging-in-Publication Data

Arluke, Arnold.
    Brute force : policing animal cruelty / Arnold Arluke.
       p. cm.
    ISBN 1-55753-350-4 (alk. paper)
    1. Animal rescue. 2. Animal welfare. I. Title.

HV4708.A755 2004
363.25'987~dc22

                2003025335

Contents

Foreword

In somewhat over a decade, sociologists have gone from essentially ignoring human/animal relationships to producing a rich body of research and writing that has begun to capture the joy, sorrow, and ambivalence that characterize this common and important form of association. Sociological human-animal studies (HAS) focus on a wide range of issues that have been central to conventional sociology and social psychology. A number of works concentrate on interspecies interaction and the unique social relationships that grow out of the routine exchanges between people and their animal coactors. Understandably, much of this literature deals with human caretakers (a.k.a., "owners") and the companion animals with which they share their daily lives (e.g., Alger and Alger 1997; Irvine 2004; Sanders 1999; Wipper 2000). Much of the literature with this focus moves beyond interaction to examine the effect of routine interspecies association on the social construction of animal mind and its impact on the social and personal identity of caretakers. Another common area of interest is animal-related social movements and the activities of movement participants directed at constructing certain aspects of the human-animal relationship as a social problem that requires solution (e.g., Herzog 1993; Jasper and Nelkin 1992; Sperling 1988) and/or how the problematic treatment of animals is related to others social problems such as inequality (e.g., Nibert 2002; Noske 1997) or human-to-human violence (e.g., Arluke 2002; Arluke and Luke 1997; Flynn 1999).

One of the most productive foci of sociological HAS involves studying the activities of those whose work involves animals. For example, researchers have explored the occupational lives of laboratory scientists (e.g., Arluke 1991; Groves 1997; Phillips 1994), shelter personnel (e.g., Alger and Alger 2003; Frommer and Arluke 1999; Irvine 2002), animal trainers (e.g., Gillespie, Leffler, and Lerner 1996; Sanders 1999, 89–110), slaughterhouse workers (e.g., Thompson 1983), and veterinarians (e.g., Bryant and Snizek 1976; Sanders 1994; Swabe 1999). Professor Arluke's *Brute Force: Animal Police and the Challenge of Cruelty* builds upon and extends this literature on animal-related work. His richly detailed and moving account of the daily lives of humane law enforcement officers reveals an occupation fraught with happiness and success, disappointment and failure, and conflict and ambiguity. Of central importance is the impact of the officers' occupational role and the routine encounters associated with it on the self-definitions and social identities of enforcement personnel. Confronted with some of the most pitiable, uncaring, and overtly cruel features of the human-animal relationship, officers must grapple with the emotional consequences of their work. Like workers in other problematic, conflict-ridden, and control-oriented occupations, they are involved in a form of "emotional labor" (Hochschild 1983). In order to do their jobs they must learn to suppress the emotions which arise from their occupational encounters in order to protect their own emotional well-being and to effectively fulfill their official functions or recognize situations in which overtly expressing emotion will lead to the resolution of problematic encounters with offenders. As Arluke emphasizes, then, the work of being a humane law enforcement officer exacts a considerable emotional toll. Officers can protect themselves by becoming insensitive to the pain and cruelty they encounter, find psychic solace in cynicism, and/or give themselves over to anger and frustration.

In addition to emotional difficulties, myriad practical problems confront Arluke's officers. They are burdened with the problem of how to define what constitutes "cruelty" and what counts as adequate evidence of this offense. In addition to distinguishing between valid and "bullshit" cases, they must decide whose account to believe. This is especially problematic in that complainants and offenders are frequently involved in conflicts that have little or nothing to do with the immediate instance of reputed animal abuse. The ambiguities are exacerbated by the variety of excuses and justifications (Hewitt and Stokes 1975; Stokes and Hewitt 1976) offered by offenders and officers' experience-based recognition that what can ostensibly be defined as abuse may not be malicious but instead may derive from offenders' ignorance, poverty, or cultural traditions. Finally, after negotiating a way across this shifting and ambiguous perceptual terrain officers must confront the problem of whether or not to intervene and, should they decide that intervention is necessary, how to effectively resolve the situation.

The occupational world of the humane officer is characterized by ambiguity. To a considerable degree this ambiguity derives from the limited and often unclear "license" attached to the work role. This mandate to carry out certain activities (see Hughes 1993, 287–292) is afforded to holders of particular occupational roles both as a formal, legally specified, element of the job and as a reputational feature–an informally conferred occupational identity–that aids the worker by affording legitimacy in the eyes of those he or she is supposed to control or serve. At best, animal police have a severely limited mandate. Both citizens and other workers in the law enforcement system regard them as nothing but "dog-catchers" or "game wardens." When they bring cases to court they find their efforts symbolically derogated as judges discount the importance of the situation ("it's only a dog") and/or apply the most minimal of sanctions. This lack of occu-pational respect and institutional support has negative impact on the experiences and perspectives of both the animal-inclined and law enforcement-oriented offi-cers depicted by Arluke. The former, who define the occupational activity as a "mission," find their ability limited to better the lot of abused animals while the latter, who typically see their occupation as a "job," find it difficult to maintain an identity as a competent enforcer of the law. Officers respond to this daily experi-ence of marginality and ineffectiveness in a variety of ways. Basically, they limit their definition of success. They define their role as simply bringing cases to court. Prosecution is seen as a form of sanctioning in itself and puts the case "on re-cord." They also see their efforts as having the value of educating both offenders and legal personnel. Offenders are "put on notice" and may take small steps to treat their animals with greater consideration while officials may come to redefine the importance of the animal-related cases and to see officers as "professionals rather than extremists."

Clearly, the work activity Professor Arluke presents in *Brute Force* is diffi-cult, disappointing, emotionally grueling, and conflict-ridden. Officers who suc-cessfully avoid cynicism or occupational burnout eventually acquire the perspec-tive that Arluke refers to as "humane realism." They bolster a positive sense of self by seeing themselves as having "the knack." Their experience has rendered them skilled in judging the key facts of cases, determining the motives of offenders and complainants, and devising practical solutions to the situations they confront.

Brute Force is the work of, arguably, the most prolific and skilled ethnog-rapher currently involved in investigating settings in which people interact with nonhuman animals. Unlike survey research, analysis of documentary evidence, or other "distanced" (a.k.a., "objective") methods typically favored by conventional sociologists, ethnography requires that the researcher directly involve himself or herself in the daily social activities of those in whom he or she is interested. Most commonly, the ethnographer enters "the field" as an inexperienced and marginal stranger (Arluke describes himself as starting out as a "rookie"). Over the months or years the ethnographer typically remains in the field, he or she ideally moves from being a newcomer to being a regular. The ethnographer becomes a well-socialized member of the group and acquires an "intimate familiarity" (Blumer 1969) with participants' perspectives, relationships, goals, routine activities, failures, and successes.

A widely acknowledged problem with studies based on surveys or formal interviews is that "subjects" (things that only royalty or researchers have) often lie, forget, selectively present, or otherwise offer versions of "reality" that have limited or, at best, unknown relationships to their actual experiences and orientations. In short, there is considerable difference between what people *say* and what they *do* (Deutscher 1973). Ethnographic research like Arluke's avoids this source of error by allowing the investigator to, in a sense, see attitudes in action. The ethnographer can use events in the field to validate, refine, and question participants' verbal accounts of the way things are and how they would act in certain circumstances (Becker and Geer 1957).

Ethnographic descriptions like the one in this book offer the reader an understanding of the social world as a *process*. They place the reader directly into the complex, ambiguous, conflictual, disappointing, and rewarding world of flesh-and-blood social actors. Had Professor Arluke based what follows simply on the available literature, interviews with humane officers, or media depictions of their work (useful, but limited, sources of information), his presentation would be quite different. Having chosen, at some level, to *become* a humane enforcement officer has allowed Arluke to construct the richly nuanced and complexly problematic description that follows.

One common critique of ethnographic methods is that, because they typically involve a small number of people who are not chosen at random, the conclusions drawn from field work are not able to be generalized. In the specific case of *Brute Force*, critics would maintain that Arluke's depiction of Massachusetts and New York humane officers does not apply to humane officers *in general*. This may, or may not, be the case. However, ethnographers counter this delegitimating critique of field methods by making two major points. First, social science is a cumulative enterprise and richly detailed descriptions based on disciplined, long-term data collection like Arluke's build upon and extend the research of others working with similar groups. Secondly, the virtue of ethnographic studies is that they provide information relevant to larger generic theoretical concerns. *Brute Force*, for example, teaches us much about such central issues as social and self identity and their relationship to one's occupation, how workers deal with problems and disappointments, the negotiation of relationships, the process of emotional labor, occupational ideology and socialization, and the maintenance of involvement in and commitment to a job (see Prus 1987).

The value of ethnographic research, then, lies not in its generalizability to large populations but, instead, in its *analytic generalizability* (see Kleinman, Copp, and Henderson 1997). The insights into identity, emotional labor, occupational ideology, and so forth provided in *Brute Force* are useful in themselves and call on us to ask, what does what we now know about the work of animal police tell us about occupational activities that have similar characteristics? After having read *Brute Force* I was most struck by the connections between the work of humane enforcers and that of conventional police officers (a group with which I have some familiarity) and child protection workers (an occupational group I was prompted to explore).

I frequently tell the students in my criminology classes that being a police officer is the most difficult job we assign to members of our society. Police are called on to be negotiators and disciplinarians, to solve and control crimes, to maintain civic order–to be helpers, authorities, social workers, and protectors. Like many jobs, police work typically is characterized by boredom and routine. However, unlike many jobs the routine of police work may, at any time, be shattered by situations that offer considerable psychic and physical danger. Further, police work entails a high degree of discretion. Patrol officers routinely make independent decisions about the "facts" of cases, how to deal with citizens, whether or not to make an arrest, and so forth. Danger and discretion combined with the fact that the police officer's job puts him or her in regular contact with some of our society's most unsavory situations and persons, give rise to what Jerome Skolnick (1994) calls the police officer's "working personality." Like the animal police described by Arluke, conventional police typically start out with a rather idealistic orientation to the job. Through experience and the socializing assistance of older officers, this initial idealism soon gives way to a more realistic perspective. Eventually, however, the daily rigors of police work commonly cause officers to become cynical, anxious, suspicious, and intolerant (Drummond 1976). Police tend to see their occupational task as maintaining order and solving immediate problems. Like humane enforcers, they employ their experience-based skills to evaluate the situation and to determine the most effective means of restoring or maintaining order (Bayley and Bittner 1984). Again, like Arluke's officers, they view arrest as a failure to negotiate order (Meehan 1992) and have little faith in the support and effectiveness of the court. A major factor that distinguishes patrol officers from humane enforcers is that the former are granted considerably more legitimacy than the latter. This lack of legitimacy is regarded by the officers in *Brute Force* (especially those with a "police orientation") as a significant disadvantage. They are called upon to do society's "dirty work" (Hughes 1993, 87–97) but are not provided with the legitimacy, authority, or institutional support they require (cf., Heinsler, Kleinman, and Stenross 1990). The fact that some humane officers acquire the perspective of "humane realism," see elements or their work as improving the lot of abused animals, and find satisfaction in their skills and insight is testimony to the resilience and commitment of those with whom Arluke worked.

Reading *Brute Force* prompted me to search out the available literature on child protection workers since the analytic connection between the job of animal police and that of social workers involved in child protection seemed obvious. The parallels in occupational experience were quite remarkable. Like humane enforcement officers, child protection workers are confronted with five major problems. First, they are burdened with the practical and statutory ambiguities surrounding the definitions of "abuse" and "neglect" (Alter 1995; Kassebaum and Chandler 1992; Munro 1996). Second, child protection workers are confronted with the problem of how to assess the "facts" of the cases to which they are assigned (Oppenheim 1992; Scott 1998). Like Arluke's animal cops, child protection workers recognize that a number of the situations brought to their attention are not valid cases of abuse. Some are unsubstantiated because they are initiated by complainants who have a malicious intent while others are invalid because the reporter misunderstands the situation and/or the severity of the alleged mistreatment (Giovannoni 1991). As a part of this activity which Arluke refers to as "shaping cases," child protectors tend to define the abuse as being due to the pathology of the suspected offender. Boushell and Lebacq (1992) advocate that child protection workers take into account some of the factors attended to by animal police–principally, the class background and culture of the offender.

Having constructed an understanding of the case, child protectors are confronted with the third problem of how to effectively intervene and how to define success (Alter 1995; Archer and Whitaker 1992; Kassenbaum and Chandler 1992). Again, the parallel with the task of animal police is readily apparent. Another linkage is seen in the potential for danger and the intense conflict that characterize case investigation and intervention. Eleven percent of the child protection workers surveyed by Horejsi and his associates (1994) had been physically assaulted on the job and 60 percent had been threatened with death or physical injury. An important difference here is that, in addition to the potential danger posed by conflicts with offenders, humane enforcers also have to cope with the threat of injury posed by some of the animals they are charged with protecting.

A final connection between the work of child protectors and animal police is seen in their similar perspectives of and relationship to the legal system with which they are, at least, nominally associated. Like humane enforcers, and enforcement personnel in general (Drummond 1976; Wilson 1973, 50-52), child protectors typically regard legal codes and restraints as problematic, see the courts as unaware of the problems they encounter on the job, and define the invalidation of cases and minimal penalties assessed as indicative of the lack of institutional support (Alexander 1995; Cooper 1992).

The consequence of these associated problems is that child protection workers must cope with anxiety, dissatisfaction, and the fear that their occupational efforts are ineffective (Fryer et al. 1988; Horowitz 1998; Morrison 1990). But despite this emotional toll, child protectors—like Arluke's animal police—incorporate elements of their on-the-job experience into their personal identities. They come to view themselves as uniquely skilled, knowledgeable, and experienced (Fryer and Miyoshi 1989; McBeath and Webb 1990-91) and retain an intense commitment to their jobs and the welfare of those they are assigned to protect (Fryer et al. 1988).

Reading *Brute Force* is not an altogether happy experience. Its pages are filled with moving accounts of some of the most egregious examples of the cruel, thoughtless, ignorant, misguided, and inhumane ways in which people treat the nonhuman animals with which they share their lives. It is, at the same time, a story of triumph and resilience. Confronted with an almost impossible task and given only minimal license and institutional support, humane enforcers, like most of us, do the best they can. They learn from their problems and disappointments and draw solace and a sense of usefulness from their successes.

Clinton R. Sanders
University of Connecticut

Acknowledgments

Many people have guided and supported my interest in animal police. Several years ago the Massachusetts Society for the Prevention of Cruelty to Animals (MSPCA) enabled me to study the relationship between animal cruelty and other forms of violence. There I met many MSPCA humane law enforcement officers and became fascinated with their mission and work. In passing, I mentioned this interest to Carter Luke, Executive Vice President for Humane Education at the "M." Luke had been an agent himself years earlier and spoke with me at length about his experience enforcing the cruelty law. Hearing this heightened my interest in studying animal police up close—as they knocked on doors, carried out investigations, and went to court. Luke never hesitated, and opened the doors of humane law enforcement for me. The President's Fund of the MSPCA made it possible for me to spend time away from teaching, immersed in the daily routine of cruelty investigation.

All the MSPCA officers and dispatchers, led by former director Walter Kilroy, were extraordinarily forthcoming and helpful. None refused my requests to drive with them, to listen and watch when they talked to complainants and respondents, or to answer the many questions I had about their work. So, too, were their New York City peers at the American Society for the Prevention of Cruelty to Animals (ASPCA), although my fieldwork at the "A" was brief by comparison. Particular thanks there to Steve Ziborowski for expediting my research.

A number of friends and colleagues read earlier drafts of this book and made suggestions that I used and implemented in the final version. Fred Hafferty, Harold Herzog, Alan Klein, Jack Levin, Claudia Mora, Trish Morris, Gary Patronek, Allan A. Rolfe, Andrew Rowan, Clint Sanders, and Ken Shapiro are all to be thanked in this regard. Jan Bober, Kara Holmquist, and Frank Martin helped me to find suitable photographs from the MSPCA's files and archives. I am grateful to Candace Cochrane for permission to use her photographs of a seized cat (p. 127) and a neglected dog (p. 13), to Dianne DeLucia for permission to use her photo of me on the dust jacket, to Patrice Flesch for permission to use her photograph of Beautiful Joe (p. 148), and to Michelle *Segall/Morning* Union (Springfield Newspapers) for permission to use her photograph of an ox pull (p. 146). Finally, thanks to Alan Beck, Jessica Burdge, and Margaret Hunt for spiriting my manuscript through the editorial process and to Lauren Rolfe for providing a sounding board and constant support along the way.

Introduction

The Rookie's Dilemma

When we hear about serious cases of cruelty, our thoughts and feelings first turn to the animal victim's plight as we contemplate their untoward experience. Our focus then turns to the person who allegedly caused this suffering, wondering what their motivations might have been to inflict such harm. This book is about neither of these concerns, at least not directly. *Brute Force* is about the impact of animal cruelty on the people who investigate these cases and prosecute abusers.

The story of humane law enforcement officers—or animal cops, as they are called—is a story of triumph, not because they reduce the frequency of cruelty or win convictions in court but because they maintain their humane sensitivities. Holding on to these sensitivities, or in some cases further sharpening them, is remarkable given the cynicism that results from endless reports of animal mistreatment that fall short of legal and departmental definitions of cruelty, frequent dismissal or denigration of their work, and constant failure to convict abusers or "make a dent" in cruelty at large. This is a story about how animal police can affirm or discover their own humaneness, despite these assaults. In the end, it is about the survival of hope for a better and just world for animals.

Special police departments devoted to enforcing animal cruelty laws strike many as a very modern concept, but they have nineteenth-century origins. Creating animal police forces followed the development of humane societies in Boston and New York. After George Angell founded the Massachusetts Society for the Prevention of Cruelty to Animals (MSPCA) and Henry Bergh the American Society for the Prevention of Cruelty to Animals (ASPCA) in 1867, they both successfully lobbied for anti-cruelty laws. Enacted in 1868 and revised in 1909, the Massachusetts animal protection law primarily focused on the abuse of horses. Although somewhat antiquated today, the code still stands. It reads:

> Whoever overdrives, overloads, drives when overloaded, overworks, tortures, torments, deprives of necessary sustenance, cruelly beats, mutilates or kills an animal, causes or procures an animal to be overdriven, overloaded, driven when overloaded, overworked, tortured or killed; and whoever uses in a cruel or inhuman manner in a race, game, or contest, or in training thereof, as lure or bait a live animal, except an animal if used as lure or bait in fishing; and whoever, having the charge or custody of an animal, either as owner or otherwise, inflicts unnecessary cruelty upon it, or unnecessarily fails to provide it with proper food, drink, shelter, sanitary environment, or protection from the weather, and whoever, as owner, possessor, or person having the charge or custody of an animal, cruelly drives or works it when unfit for labor, or willfully abandons it, or carries it or causes it to be carried in or upon a vehicle, or otherwise, in an unnecessarily cruel or inhuman manner or in a way and manner which might endanger the animal carried thereon, or knowingly, and willfully authorizes or permits it to be subjected to unnecessary torture, suffering or cruelty of any kind shall be punished by a fine of not more than one thousand dollars or by imprisonment for not more than one year, or both. In addition to any other penalty provided by law, upon conviction for any violation of this section . . . the defendant may, after an appropriate hearing to determine the defendant's fitness for continued custody of the abused animal, be ordered to surrender or forfeit . . . the animal whose treatment was the basis of such conviction. [Chapter 272, Section 77]

To enforce this law, and its parallel in New York, the MSPCA and the ASPCA created small police departments within their organizations. Little is known about the nature of early animal police work other than what has been recorded in the annual reports of humane societies having such departments. For the most part, these brief records only note the numbers and kinds of cases prosecuted by officers. Humane agents, empowered as police officers, primarily investigated cruelty to horses, since the urban infrastructure required these animals to be well tended and healthy. One typical entry catalogued the ASPCA's work in New York (ASPCA 1883); agents carried out 768 prosecutions, 446 specifically involving the mistreatment of horses for offenses such as beating, abandoning, starving, overloading, driving until they fell dead, and working sick, lame, or worn-out horses. Other prosecutions involved dog and cockfighting, rat baiting, feeding cows swill and garbage, keeping cows in filthy condition, refusing to relieve cows with distended udders, cruelty to cattle, dogs, cats, and poultry, and maliciously killing, mutilating, and wounding animals with knives and other instruments. The only other information is the rare commentary about the work of humane law enforcement agents. In one case (ASPCA 1867, 28), the report noted how "discouraging" it was for agents to be criticized for "overzealousness."

By the middle of the twentieth century, the makeup and organization of humane law enforcement departments in cities like Boston and New York resembled their present-day form. The MSPCA's department is made up of sixteen staff members, including eleven investigative officers, a consulting veterinarian, two dispatchers, and a director and assistant director. Except for the dispatchers, all have been appointed as

A neglected puppy awaits a physical examination. At this age and in this condition, the puppy is unlikely to survive.

Special State Police Officers by the State of Massachusetts, although they are restricted to the enforcement of animal protection laws and regulations. They do, however, conduct investigations, obtain and execute search warrants, make arrests, and sign and prosecute complaints. Officers are assigned throughout the state to investigate whether individuals and, less often, organizations, have been cruel or neglectful. The bulk of their cases involve "everyday" animals—the strays, pets, vermin, and small-farm livestock—that are neglected or sometimes deliberately mistreated by individuals. They also visit and inspect stockyards, slaughterhouses, race tracks, pet shops, guard dog businesses, hearing ear dog businesses,

An inspector surveys the horses and facilities at a race track.

horse stables that rent or board horses, kennels, and animal dealers licensed by the United States Department of Agriculture. During a typical year, MSPCA officers conduct approximately 5,000 investigations and 1,000 inspections, involving more than 150,000 animals (Kilroy 1991). Since such complaints are also lodged with other organizations in the state, estimates of abuse complaints easily surpass 10,000 annually in Massachusetts and show evidence of steadily mounting over time.

According to their official job description (MSPCA 1995), the primary purpose of officers' work is "to prevent cruelty to animals, to relieve animal suffering, and to advance the welfare of animals whenever and wherever possible. Such purposes are to be achieved through the pursuit and implementation of a combination of activities, including, but not necessarily limited to, the enforcement of Massachusetts anti-cruelty and related laws, and the dissemination of animal protection/welfare related information." To do this work, prospective employees are expected to have a number of skills, the first of which is "humane sensitivity, with affinity for, and ability to empathize with animals and respond with compassion and objectivity."

When investigating cruelty complaints, rookie officers think of themselves as a brute force because they believe that they have legitimate authority to represent the interests of abused animals. They see themselves as a power for the helpless, a voice for the mute, representing and speaking for animals when their welfare or lives are in jeopardy. With more time on the job, this view changes. Although they are expected to represent the animal's "side" when investigating cruelty complaints, officers encounter a number of problems that make it difficult to do this. For the rookie officer fresh from the academy, these problems can be confusing and discouraging. Hired in part because of their "humane sensitivity," this strong concern for animals plus their recent police training creates a number of expectations in them. Rookies expect to handle complaints against animals that violate the legal definition of cruelty as well as their own standards, to observe animals to ascertain the nature and extent of cruelty, to counsel "respondents" when necessary to improve the treatment of their animals, to prosecute those respondents who commit egregious acts of cruelty or who do not comply with advice, and to be understood and respected as both police and humane officers. These expectations are quickly disappointed as rookies begin investigating complaints.

First, professional identity is a problem. Rookie officers experience a disparity between how they see themselves and how others see them. On the one hand, officers see themselves as professional law enforcers and animal protectors. As one officer said of the department's general job expectation: "They want you to be a humane officer, but have the authority or the presence of a police officer. It's hard to do both." On the other hand, one reason why it is "hard to do both" is that friends, family, strangers, and other professionals often are confused by this combination and either have no idea what humane officers do or relegate them to the level of "dogcatcher."

Second, officers must enforce a problematic law. Massachusetts, like other states, has an anti-cruelty code specifying that animals should not be deliberately mistreated. The law prohibits many types of abuse and neglect that threaten the safety and well-being of animals, including but not limited to beating, mutilating, or killing them as well as failing to provide them with proper food, drink, and protection from the weather (Fennessy n.d.). Those convicted of violating this law can be fined up to $1,000 and imprisoned for as long as one year or both. Additional animal protection laws classified as felonies have increased the maximum prison sentence to five years.

Despite the existence of the law, officers find it difficult to enforce because of vague use of terms such as "neglect," "abuse," "proper care," "necessary veterinary care," and "suffering." Nor can officers fall back on more general cultural conceptions of suffering, since these, too, are vague and contested by different groups. This problem forces officers to interpret the meaning and application of the law on a case by case basis, a point aptly made by the former director of the department (Kilroy n.d.), who noted the "continuing absence of a widely accepted definition of cruelty to animals. Every activity that threatens the well-being of animals . . . must be challenged and overcome on a largely individual basis."

Third, there is a problem with evidence. The best witness to the abuse of humans is the victim; their testimony certainly facilitates, although does not guarantee, successful prosecution. Yet animals obviously cannot report or articulate

5

their harm. Rookies must learn how to figure out whether an animal has been mistreated, relying on indirect evidence in order to "tell the story" of an act of abuse. Rookies discover that a large part of this indirect evidence comes from investigating humans. In fact, this human side of animal cruelty often becomes the deciding factor in handling and resolving complaints.

Finally, there is a problem with enforcement and prosecution. Rookies encounter very few clear-cut cases of animal cruelty that lead to prosecution and punishment. Instead, they encounter respondents whose behavior toward their animals does not violate the law, but falls short of what officers would prefer to see. Without a technical violation of the cruelty law, officers feel that they have little, if any, authority to force respondents to improve their treatment of animals. When they meet respondents whose acts violate the law, officers see their advice ignored. Rather than giving up entirely at these times, rookies must learn how to get their message across to respondents and, if necessary, take them to court. This final option also can be particularly frustrating, especially for rookies, as they encounter a judicial system that seems indifferent or hostile to the concerns of animals.

How can rookies combat cruelty in the face of complaints having little, if anything, to do with cruelty and animals who cannot tell their story of abuse? How can they feel effective as humane law enforcement officers in the face of respondents who ignore their suggestions and courts that deflate their authority? How can they feel respected as humane law enforcement officers in the face of public and professional people who do not understand or ridicule their work? In total, these frustrations challenge the sensibilities of rookies and threaten their initial idealism and humane sensitivity. The question, then, is not merely to ask how officers learn to cope with these assaults to their humane sensitivity, but to ask what replaces it over time.

Method

I, too, was a rookie. I became an ethnographer of the world of humane law enforcement to understand how animal cruelty complaints were managed. As an outsider, my goal was to capture the shared perspective of officers and dispatchers toward their work. Like any newcomer, I had to figure out how to act when investigating respondents suspected of cruelty, what to think about "complainants" who seemed to have unreasonable expectations for enforcing the law, and how to feel when "obvious" and strong cases came up short in court. Like any rookie, I wanted to know how others thought, felt, and behaved on the job to understand my experiences, guide my reactions, and measure my responses.

As a "naive" outsider I knew little about humane law enforcement other than what I read in the press by journalists and public relations experts. Most of these reports were human interest stories that gave a quick glimpse of cruelty work by profiling a single officer. Two of the better ones featured an officer from the MSPCA (Scocca 1997) and from the ASPCA (Galvin 1998), but I suspected that their work, and the adaptations they made to it, were far more complex and interesting than could be spelled out in a few pages. I had a similar reaction to the only book about animal police, *Fifty Years in the Doghouse* (Alexander 1963), an account of one agent's work during the first half of the twentieth century in New York City. Some time after I stopped my fieldwork, television gave the public a close look at the work of animal cops. As a form of "edutainment," the Animal Planet channel airs weekly broadcasts of a handful of animal cops carrying out carefully selected investigations in New York and Detroit.

Of course, as a sociologist I had a certain way of seeing the world of cruelty investigation. I am always drawn to looking at how people make sense of and manage new experiences and problems, a universal social process regardless of particular group membership (Prus 1997). Like any kind of work, new cruelty workers undergo a transformation as they encounter problems with no obvious or already learned solution. They turn to experienced colleagues for direction, learning how to rationalize and explain certain things, minimize frustration and anger, and come to think about themselves in positive ways.

As an ethnographer, I wanted to witness these transformations so I could understand why they occurred and how they affected dispatchers and officers. To do this, I immersed myself in the world of fighting cruelty. I spent six months with the MSPCA's law enforcement staff in the office and in the field, interviewing and observing sixteen people, including three dispatchers, eleven officers, the assistant director, and the director. These observations and interviews produced about seven hundred pages of transcriptions and notes.

I was careful to explain my research to department members before meeting them as well as when I met them in person. More than one officer seemed concerned that my observations might harm them in some way. A few were worried that things they said might "get back to the wrong people" and get them in trouble. Others wondered if my conclusions would lead to job cuts or other unwanted changes at work, since they claimed that this happened once before with someone who observed them. I, of course, described the steps I would take to ensure the confidentiality of complainants, respondents, and department members. I told them that my writing would not use their real names or any details about them that could lead to their identification. When in the field, I also made it clear to officers that I would never tape their conversations with complainants and respondents. However, with their permission, I recorded my interviews with them for later analysis.

The interviews started the moment I spoke with officers to set up meetings or ride-along and ended as I said goodbye to them at the end of the day or, in a few cases, after they called me at home to provide additional information. I was guided by a general interview instrument that sought to capture their perspective toward humane law enforcement. But as an open-ended guide, I quickly found that my conversations with officers went beyond the confines of the instrument. Officers were allowed to construct an agenda around their concerns and the cases we investigated as I probed for the meaning of their words and experiences and searched for unanticipated but useful leads. I used a similar approach to talk with dispatchers and others.

Because I conducted these interviews while department members performed their jobs, I could observe dispatchers interact with officers and callers, and watch officers interact with complainants, respondents, neighbors, animal control officers, and regular police. I watched dispatchers handle callers making animal complaints and observed officers investigate cases. I escorted officers as they left their cars and knocked on respondents' doors, so I could observe how complaints were managed. Usually, officers introduced me as an "observer" or said nothing about my presence as the interaction unfolded. In almost all cases, respondents ignored me and focused their attention on officers. Only one respondent asked who I was; if others turned to me, it was only to make brief eye contact as they told their stories of caring for their animals. I always went home to write detailed field notes about my experiences.

What do these interviews and observations represent? Certainly, they do not offer an "objective" view of humane law enforcement work. Dispatchers and officers would talk about what they personally believed I needed to know. Predictably, problematic and unexpected occurrences found their way into conversation more than did unproblematic and routine happenings. That this happened is not unique to studying humane law enforcement workers, nor is it methodologically undesirable. The converse, however, would be a problem.

It is also reasonable to assume that officers were on their "best behavior" as I rode with them to investigate complaints. However, several factors made me believe that what I saw and heard accurately reflected the world of humane law enforcement. First, while I rode for a single day with each officer, I was with them for a long time. Riding alone with them for many hours created an almost ideal interview "chamber" that made it possible for most, if not all, officers to feel some rapport with me and to be comfortable talking about their work-related experiences and plans, their likes and dislikes, and their hopes and fears. Of course, some officers appeared to drop their guard more quickly and talk freely, while others took longer to do so. But with all of them, there were many indicators telling me that I could trust their words and see their acts as genuine. For instance, several officers initiated discussions of what I felt were sensitive matters without my prodding them. One example of this was officers who spontaneously talked about why they felt it was sometimes necessary and appropriate to trespass on the respondents' property during investigations. It was also common for officers to say that they liked having me ride with them and enjoyed talking to me about their work, since they typically had no one to talk to other than respondents.

There also is the question of generalization. To what extent, if at all, does the experience of department members apply to other humane officers and dispatchers around the country? Although the department examined in this report is part of the MSPCA, I believe that little of what I say is unique to that organization and its humane law enforcement workers in terms of the kinds of problems they face on the job and the solutions they create. Indeed, I spent six weeks in New York City with the ASPCA's humane law enforcement department, and those 16 officers and dispatchers reported the same thoughts, feelings, and experiences I heard in Boston, except for differing details that did not alter the larger picture. I would prefer that the reader think of what follows as a description and analysis of a particular job, and then compare it to the experience of law enforcement workers elsewhere, not merely those who enforce the cruelty code.

1

Pecking Order

> I'm not a paint thrower or anything like that [animal rights activist]. But let's get this straight, I love animals. I have a dog. I'd run through fire for him. But am I one of these people who is going to break into somebody's property for a dog with no shelter that is healthy just because my heart tells me . . . ? If I arrested everybody because of my heart, half of Queens would be locked up.

Animal police are often maligned by friends, family, strangers, and regular police officers. They are negatively stereotyped as "dogcatchers," "extremists," or animal control workers. Disparaging views like these conflict with how officers see themselves as professional police who combat the important problem of animal cruelty. Their response is to assert an occupational identity that is a distinct and vital form of both police and animal work.

In practice it is difficult for most officers to emphasize both, although they strive to blend the two. To some extent, police and animal work, while not contradictory, draw on different values and call forth different interests in officers. Nevertheless, the department manages to anchor its identity to police and animal work by not expecting officers to have an equal commitment to both orientations and by distancing itself from the group to which it is most commonly and negatively confused—animal control. These unofficial organizational strategies combine potentially conflicting roles into one work identity.

Judging Animal Police

Some people understood and applauded the work of animal police, especially family and friends. A few officers had spouses who served as veterinary nurses, shelter technicians, or law enforcement dispatchers and knew firsthand what animal police did. Others had parents, siblings, or children who respected the goals of humane law enforcement. A few had friends who praised their work. For instance, one officer claimed that his childhood friends had a positive reaction when they discovered what he did for a living: "'Hey, I'm a cop for animals.' 'You're a cop? Does that mean that you can arrest people?' When I said, 'Yeah, for animal abuse,' it was, 'That's cool, that's cool.'" Despite this occasional support, usually outsiders did not understand their work or worse, deliberately demeaned it.

Dogcatchers

Officers were commonly seen as glorified "dogcatchers" or perhaps "cat rescuers." Sometimes they would write off these degrading labels as mere teasing. As one officer said of his brother, "It's good-natured teasing. They'll say, 'Aw, you're nothing but a dogcatcher.' You get that from different people." More often, such comments were mean-spirited and barbed.

Regular police, in particular, often dismissed humane officers, ridiculing more than just teasing them for being dogcatchers. "They're not going to treat us like professionals. They are going to treat us like dogcatchers. You can get that feeling right away when you walk into a police station and they say, 'Call the dog officer.' We go to the same academy they go to and we'd help them out," lamented an officer. This demeaning attitude could be encountered when visiting a local police department. Before entering the District Five station, Officer Hal* said that he "hated" going in because of the frequent "cracks and comments." He had been told on prior visits never to step behind the receiving counter because only "real cops" could do that. Standing in front of this counter, Hal said, "I'm here to meet Sally Smith." Getting on the intercom, the regular police officer behind the desk announced, "Woof, woof, your doggy guy is here." After returning to his car,

---

* All human and animal names have been changed to protect the anonymity of participants.

Hal slumped in his seat and said, "I was like, 'Hey, thanks buddy. Call me when you're in a jam.'" Similarly, barking sounds over a microphone greeted another member of the department when a police squad car pulled up next to his humane law enforcement vehicle, as pedestrians looked on from the sidewalk.

Others put down humane law enforcers by confusing them with animal control workers. Several officers reported friends whose confusion disparaged their work, as in the following case: "My good friends, like from college and stuff, they still don't understand what I do. They introduce me like, 'This is my friend the cat cop.' People are like, 'What do you do, rescue cats out of trees?'" Even though such comments were usually unintentional, officers still found them to be denigrating and disturbing. As one said, "Yeah, when someone says, 'Are you animal control?' I say, 'No, I'm MSPCA.' I have a real problem with being called animal control." Officers usually corrected these misinformed and insulting remarks. One made sure to distinguish cruelty work from mere animal control: "People come up to me and ask questions. Some are stupid. A lot of times they say, 'Oh, the dogcatcher's here.' You got a mouthful of food and, you know, 'Sorry to bother you, but there's this dog in my neighborhood . . .' Then you say, 'I'm not the dogcatcher. I'm a cruelty investigator. I usually don't pick up animals. That is someone else's function.'" Another went further by specifying the kind of animal mistreatment investigated and prosecuted by humane law enforcement: "They think we are animal control or a dog officer, and we are there because their dog is barking. They will go into this twenty-five minute litany . . . 'But Mrs. Smith's dog barks all the time, and so-and-so's dog barks all the time.' Then I'll tell them, 'I don't care if your dog barks or your neighbor's dog barks. I'm here because your dog is being mistreated. It is skinny and has no shelter.'"

An officer investigates the case of a neglected dog without food, water, and shelter.

And others confused officers with environmental police, fish and game wardens, park rangers, or occupations having nothing to do with animals. For example, while standing in downtown Boston, one officer was approached by out-of-town tourists who opened a map of historic sites in the area and asked him for advice on what to visit. He politely demurred and pointed them to a nearby park ranger whose uniform, except for the brimmed hat, was very similar to those worn by MSPCA law enforcement staff. Another officer was mistaken as an employee of the state's environmental police department as she stopped to pay a toll on the turnpike. "Oh, you're with environmental," matter-of-factly said the collector. "No, I'm with the MSPCA—prevention of cruelty," she replied. The collector responded: "Oh, you're the people who hate hunting." Making the final comment before driving off, the officer said, "No, we're not. We would prefer another way, but we don't want to see the suffering." And on rare occasions, a few officers were mistaken for security or delivery personnel. One claimed that he was confused with a UPS delivery man, saying, "I like what I do and I feel comfortable with what I do until I hear some comment that shouldn't affect me, but it does."

Officers saw their work denigrated more indirectly. For example, egregious cruelty, usually involving dogs, seemed to "count" to outsiders like regular police. Sometimes they were concerned enough about these extreme cases to investigate them if they were something "like the dog was shot up or poisoned." However, they drew a sharp line between these dramatic and disturbing incidents and all other abuse and neglect cases, like "no shelter," which accounted for the vast majority of humane officers' workload. The latter were disregarded by regular police and referred to humane law enforcement or animal control. An officer said that one police department gave "me all these stupid little picayune cat complaints and stuff, and it turned out the cops were handling this one and that one [cruelty cases]." Since much of their work was not seen as serious enough for police to investigate, officers concluded that by implication other kinds of animal mistreatment must be viewed inconsequentially.

Even more dismissive to officers, other police departments refused to handle any kind of cruelty case, regardless of its nature. In District Three, it's "'Hey, it's animal abuse . . . get it out of here, give it to the MSPCA.' They don't want to bother with it, deal with it, know about it." As a new officer said of her brief experience with police, "I've had some real bad experiences with them. 'We don't deal with dogs.' I'd like to say, 'It's animal cruelty. It's on the books—you enforce it.' But you can't really say that to them. They just don't think it's important enough for them." Indeed, regular police might not even refer these cases to humane law enforcement. "Usually they refer everything to animal control. If it involves an animal, they say, 'Call animal control' and brush it right off," said an officer.

Extremists

If not dogcatchers, then humane officers were perceived as extremists with unreasonable expectations of how animals should be treated. They frequently got this message from regular police; as one officer said, "In some of the towns, they [police] just think we are idiots—we're way off base—we're animal rights type people—not in the real world." Another officer recalled the following incident: "I ran into a police officer and he saw a bunch of our people at court. And he said, 'Gee, I didn't even know you guys [activists] had cops until I saw you at court. I thought you were back-of-the-woods, tree-hugging do-gooders.'"

Environmental police also saw them as extremists, according to officers working in rural parts of the state. While some humane officers developed cordial working relationships with individual environmental police, others felt accused of "making a big deal" over animal cruelty. Two officers, for example, found violations in the treatment and handling of crows and pigeons being used to make a movie. When they visited the nearby environmental police office, "they laughed us out of there because there's basically an open season on crows. 'You can go out and shoot them any time you want, so why are you making a big deal about these crows?' And we contacted federal people because they're migratory birds, but they didn't give a damn. We took a lot of harassment." Another officer noted, "I mean, environmental police feel like the MSPCA is trying to outlaw everything that's their job. Like we banned traps and the next thing you know we're going to stop hunting. Next thing you know we are going to stop fishing. That's their outlook on it."

To officers, the extremist image meant that they had the wrong priorities. Zealousness per se was not criticized when people were helped, but enthusiastic efforts to aid animals were belittled. This happened to Officer Tom during an investigation of a boy beating his dog. After two visits, he did not see either the dog or the boy, so he went to the local Quarrytown police department for assistance. Speaking to a Quarrytown lieutenant, Tom said, "Look, this is the situation. I was wondering, while you guys are patrolling, if you guys could just take a peek over there and see if you see the dog maybe, and get me some information on the kid." The lieutenant replied sternly: "Hey pal, what are we, the fuckin' puppy police? Let me tell you something. We have outstanding warrants for home invasion and stuff like that that we can't execute. You want me to go harass some kid for beating on his dog? We've got better things to do." If their priorities were confused, then protecting animals was "going overboard." One officer saw this attitude in his father's reaction to humane law enforcement work: "He doesn't get protecting animals. Protecting people is a noble job. People need protection. They're civilization. Animals, well, they're things for people to own or possess or use, and no one should mistreat them. He doesn't think that an entire police department should be dedicated to helping animals—that we go a little overboard for protection. He doesn't look at it as though helping animals is important."

Ironically, while officers were accused of caring too much for animals, they occasionally got the opposite reaction; namely, that they did not care very much about them if they could investigate cruelty and see such suffering. Presumably, only a hardened person, or one that never cared about animals, could do their work. They got this message from wives or husbands who, after hearing or seeing the details of a cruelty investigation, became upset. As one officer noted, "My wife

doesn't mind hearing about things, for the most part, but she will sometimes say, 'Gee, I don't want to look at those pictures.' Or I'll be doing paperwork before dinner and I'll say, 'Hey, take a look at these.' 'Oh no, I really don't want to look at them before we eat dinner.'" According to officers, the message was that companions were glad that someone did this work, but they could not do it because they were

Cruelty officers learn to view such sights as this dog, left to freeze to death, without becoming unduly upset.

more sensitive to suffering. This view offended many officers who believed that their humane sensibilities exceeded those of most people, and that they could still care about animals even if their work did not upset them. This left animal police feeling like other "dirty workers" (Hughes 1964) whose jobs society deems necessary, but then castigates or stigmatizes them for doing.

Officers responded by not talking about the details of their work unless asked, a technique shared with other workers who find that people would rather not know specifics about their jobs (Arluke 1991). As one said, "I never bring my job home unless they have questions or are interested in something or heard something. I'll talk about anything they want, but I won't on my own just start discussing what's going on with my job after supper." When they talked about bad cases, they did so rather vaguely. For example, one officer said while his family showed interest in hearing about "serious" cases, he learned to respond in very general terms. And in a few instances, they claimed that significant others did not want to hear anything about their work. In one case, the officer said of her mother: "She is very supportive, the most loving woman in the world, she would do anything for me. But she doesn't want to hear about my job. It really bothers her." In another case where a respondent beat to death an animal, the officer said: "I can't tell my wife what happened because she'll be like, 'Unbelievable—that poor dog. The dog was probably looking at him, wagging his tail and then he hit it.'" Similarly, a colleague could not tell her husband about cases. She noted, "My husband and I don't talk about my work at all. He gets very upset about it. He likes animals as much as I do but he can't stand it. He can watch stupid things on TV like operations, but he can't watch a dog sitting in a pile of trash. So we just don't talk. I'll tell him about the people I deal with rather than the animals."

While officers politely avoided talking to many outsiders about their worst cases, this occupational etiquette had deeper significance. It ironically was one small factor among many that furthered the larger problem of being improperly understood and granted little legitimacy as police. By only talking with fellow officers about their most disturbing cases, the most police-like incidents that might involve the use of force, firearms, or prosecution went unnoticed. The perception that animal police must be dogcatchers or extremists could easily stand, making for a precarious connection between humane law enforcement and regular police. They could not be "real cops" because they *just* did animal work. As one said of his father, "I think that to this day, he doesn't think it's police work. He's like, 'When are you going to get a real cop job?'" Another officer said of regular police: "They are like, 'The dog police.' There's always going to be those that are like, 'You're not a real cop.'" And another officer more generally bemoaned: "It's sort of everybody is like, 'When are you going to become a real cop?' And you just get sick of hearing that." Part of the challenge of cruelty was for officers to manage this ambiguous if not discredited identity.

Dividing

Although officers were often reminded of this disparaging view, they did not accept it; instead they carved out an occupational identity that anchored cruelty work to regular policing. They did this by having two competing humane law enforcement perspectives. This structure is not a unique organizational form. Organizations are rarely composed of a single homogeneous culture. Occupational subcultures commonly exist that differ from the overall organizational culture, either intensifying its understandings and practices or diverging from them (Trice and Beyer 1993). The essential characteristic of these groups is the self-definition of members rather than an organizationally conferred job title or official distinction (Van Maanen and Barley 1984). As part of their consciousness of kind, each subculture shares its own beliefs, values, and norms which develop as members look to each other for confirmation of the meanings they ascribe to events around them and for approval of the behaviors they prefer and espouse (e.g., Hebden 1975).

Officers' consciousness of kind expressed itself in two ways. They saw each other as leaning toward either the police or animal side of cruelty work, and they presented themselves to colleagues and the public accordingly. One officer, for instance, compared herself to a colleague when first meeting strangers: "Officer Kelly would say, 'I help animals out. I'm in humane law enforcement.' I would tell people that 'I'm a police officer that specializes in animal investigations.'" While apparently minor and superficial, such differences had deeper significance for their identities as humane law enforcement officers and for the functioning of the department. A tension existed between animal-inclined officers who saw their work as a mission and police-oriented peers who saw their work as just a job.

Just a Job

The possibility of doing police work drew many rookies to this job, having worked earlier as regular police or having grown up in families where others served in this field. As one humane officer said: "I started out being more attracted to the law enforcement aspect of it. I still to this day like that part. I've always . . . when you're really young, you think about what you want to do for your whole life. Police work always entered my mind." This was true for one officer, who, like some of her colleagues, worked part time for a local police department. On the way to investigate a case in an inner-city dwelling, she reflected: "You're walking up, and if you think that something might happen, you get that sort of adrenaline rush. I hate to say it, but I like that rush." These officers also liked the powers and trap-pings associated with regular police work. For one officer, it was having the legal authority to make arrests "for our own protection. If we get assaulted or if we come across a situation, such as a gun or somebody has a switchblade, something like that." For another, it was wanting a siren on his MSPCA vehicle to indicate emergencies, as well as "blue lights" to transport prisoners or to park in hazardous areas, much like the ASPCA squad cars.

For these police-oriented officers, humane law enforcement was a job. One they would work hard at, always conducting themselves as "professionals," but never becoming "radicals" on a mission. As one such officer said, "I mean, my life doesn't revolve around animals. It's my job to step in if I see somebody being cruel to an animal. I don't want to be seen as a crusader because I don't want to be labeled as a radical. I don't want any part of that. I just want to be categorized as a professional in my work. If I see an animal cruelty violation, I will prosecute if I can."

By viewing their roles this way, these officers managed their feelings by re-stricting, minimizing, or denying the impact of cruelty on their mental and emo-tional states, a practice shared with regular police who are trained to detach their feelings and behave in an unemotional manner (Violanti 1981). Some did this by drawing sharp boundaries between what they felt at work and what they allowed themselves to feel at home. Since it was a job and not a mission, they rarely "took their work home." One officer explained, "I don't think I ever went home and cried. I mean, it's never affected my life in a negative way. I've always taken my paperwork, and that kind of thing. The logistics of the job I've taken home, but I can honestly say I've never gone home and felt bad because that poor dog's out in the rain. I feel bad about that, but I haven't taken that home." Others managed their emotions at work by not personalizing investigations. They often spoke about remaining "objective," a code word for not being perceived as an animal rights activist or "fanatic," as the following officer made clear: "You can't allow your personal beliefs or feelings to affect the way you do your job because if you do that you start to lose your objectivity. And you get to the point where you ei-ther drive yourself nuts, and you can't do the job, or you become totally ineffec-tive. There are a lot of things that I believe personally but I try, and sometimes it's difficult, to not let personal feelings or attitudes get involved." Another officer talked about how he focused on respondents' legal infractions rather than experi-encing cases "personally." He noted, "I don't think you can take the job too personally. Yeah, it bothers me, but I don't think I could take everything personally—go after people that way. You have to kind of keep an open mind and say, 'Okay, this is the complaint I got and does it violate the law—yes or no?' "

Because they managed their emotions, police-oriented officers accepted that their personal standards for treating animals should not be imposed on others, as long as people provided minimally acceptable care under the law. One officer described how he saw his own animals: "I take care of my animals as well as some people take care of their kids. I think probably anyone that works for the MSPCA is a little on the extreme side of how they care for their animals. My dogs, we have them in the house. We treat them as part of the family." Yet he acknowledged that not everyone included animals as part of their family, but that would be acceptable if proper care was provided. "In the general public, that generally isn't the case. But that doesn't mean that you can't treat them the best way possible. I don't feel that just because someone's going to raise an animal for food and kill it doesn't mean that they don't take good care of their animals and feel for them. It's just how it is." However, in their opinion, animal-inclined colleagues did a disservice to the department because they could not live with this disparity, expecting respondents to provide the same standard of care that they did. One department member summed up this criticism:

> You have some people who work for us, and some of them are excellent, but you can't take every dog home and cuddle it. You can't expect every complaint you go on for them to take their dogs to bed like you do, or to have them all wrapped up in rosy . . . you can't. People aren't going to do it. And if you go out there with every case thinking you're going to get that done, some people will say, "Get the 'F' out of here. It's my dog. I'll leave him out there if I want to leave him out there. And I'll feed him when I want." Like you go out there and somebody is feeding their dog table scraps, somebody will say, "Well, you can't feed him that." And it's like, where in the law does it say you can't feed him that? Come on, common sense comes in. There's a lot of people that just don't have common sense. You can't go in there with your emotions flowing.

In short, they believed that by improperly managing their emotions, animal-inclined colleagues allowed their work to become a mission.

Unchecked emotions meant jeopardizing relationships with local police departments because "fanatical" animal-inclined colleagues could not "play the game" with law enforcement authorities. One police-oriented officer explained the problem created by their "unrealistic" colleagues: "Some of them really have a hard time playing the game. If I'm dealing with a police department and the police say, 'Aw, it's just a stupid dog complaint . . . da, da, da,' you can't sit there and start pissing and moaning. 'But this dog wasn't cared for properly and this and that.' You lose your credibility with the police department." He claimed that one should play the police game in the following way: "So you say, 'I know what you're talking about, but over the scope of things . . .' and you try and educate them. Or you joke along with them if you need to. Some of our people really have a problem dealing with that. But you have to do that because if you don't you come across too fanatical. If you come across as though you're off in left field, people just look at you and you don't get any help. Nothing." Instead, police-oriented officers felt that it was important not to be seen as a "wacko." As one said: "They [police] realize that I'm not a wacko—pushing that the animals have these rights and all that. I'm reasonable and we can work together."

Unchecked emotions could limit their effectiveness in court, according to police-oriented staff, because animal-inclined officers could not be "objective" or "professional," and therefore would not be taken seriously by officials. They were doomed to fail in court because they had unreasonable expectations and lacked "common sense." As one police-oriented officer said of them: "You have to convince them that an ordinary guy in the street would look at that and say, 'That's cruelty or that shouldn't be done.' With a horse, if you expect him to have a foot of shavings in the stall, they're not going to accept that. I think that everyone that works has to have humane sensitivity for animals, but you also have to have common sense too." Having such expectations doomed animal-inclined officers in court when they expressed themselves, claimed police-oriented peers: "I think it affects their credibility in the court system. If we are perceived as an animal rights group, I don't think we can function as we do today."

Unchecked emotions also compromised the public's view of humane law enforcement, "making us look like a bunch of nuts," asserted police-oriented officers. "The way I look at this department, you can't have people take you seriously if you think you are too extreme. I don't like people looking at me as though I'm an extreme animal rights person," insisted one officer. According to some, further "radicalization" endangered the department because this would alter public perception of the entire humane society. The latter should be perceived, police-oriented officers argued, as a "level ground" between abusers and activists. As one officer cautioned, "Some people have problems differentiating organizations like ours that have 'animal protection' type people and organizations that have 'animal rights' type people or people who tend to be more radical." If the humane society is perceived as an "animal rights" group, these officers believed that people would see them as "very fanatical, very unrealistic," and the organization would be "stigmatized." As an example, one officer expressed concern about how the public perceived a peer who was a vegetarian and a member of an animal rights organization: "Officer Helen is a vegetarian. I don't think there are any problems with that, but I think if she was out in the field and told people that she was a vegetarian or she's working for an animal rights group, that could block her. If she told a farmer that she had a complaint on him, in his mind, she's just an animal rights person and that's going to create a problem."

Finally, unchecked emotions lead to inappropriate case work, according to police-oriented members of the department. They argued that animal-inclined officers' unrealistic expectations ignored the realities faced by respondents and their inability to change behavior. One cited the example of pet store complaints investigated by officers having "very strong opinions" that "slant the way they do their job" and made them "unrealistic as far as what they want the pet shop to do." They were no longer "objective," in this officer's words. By contrast, he insisted that pet stores have regulations that must be followed and that the department could not "get very picayune about different things. You've got to realize that there are a lot of times that things just don't go the way you want them to go. Maybe the place didn't get cleaned as good as it should have because they were short on help and it didn't get done in a timely a fashion. Obviously, you go there at ten o'clock in the morning, the place isn't going to be spotless. At two o'clock in the afternoon, probably it should be." Another elaborated this view: "Say, for instance, someone is leaving their dog out twenty-four hours a day tied to a dog house. When I had dogs, my dogs weren't tied out to a dog house twenty-four hours a day. That goes against what I personally believe. But the law allows them, if they comply with the law, to have their dogs out as long as they are caring for them properly. And whether I agree with something or not, doesn't even come into play. What comes into play is whether it's a violation of the law." The former officer did not expect to make respondents behave differently because their attitudes were thought to be intractable. "Generally people's attitudes are made up," proclaimed another officer. Continuing, he said: "You're not going to change a guy's attitude on Maple Street about how he cares for his dog. It's highly unlikely. They're grown-up adults. They're not going to change. You can get frustrated trying to get someone to play with their dog and take it in, but if they are not going to do it, and it's not a violation of the law not to do it, what are you going to do? There's nothing you can do."

Police-oriented officers felt that the emotionality of animal-inclined officers made them too aggressive with respondents. One officer explained: "I've always loved animals and I've always wanted to help them, but I know that you can't overstep your boundaries. You can't be a fanatic. Take care of the animal. Give the animal all of its proper needs. And yes, if you can get a little more from the person by doing this and doing that, kind of work with it, but don't make it—'You should do this and you should do that.' Say, 'Well, it would be nice if you had this or you had that or if you could do this or that.'" This alleged "aggressiveness," according to police-oriented officers, meant that animal-inclined colleagues lacked "good judgment" about when to intervene in cases, reacting too quickly to perceived "suffering" in animals. One officer expressed this view: "You've got to realize when there's no more you can do until things either get worse or you can prosecute the individual. You can't take it home. You can't be going to the house every day bugging them. It's just a waste of time. That's when you've really got to have good judgment and when it gets bad enough, do something about it. A lot of people can't accept that. 'I gotta do something now because the animal's suffering.' It might be, but what are you going to do?"

By contrast, police-oriented officers claimed not to allow their own beliefs to interfere with the proper investigation of complaints. Rather than being aggressive with respondents, they took a less confrontational approach. For example, in cases that were not clear-cut legal violations, they adopted a wait-and-see policy before pressuring people for changes. In one illustrative no-shelter complaint, the officer said nothing to the respondent about tying his dog under a tree or building a doghouse because the weather was pleasant. In his words, "If he had the dog out with no shade for an extended period of time when the weather is hot—and I wouldn't consider the weather too hot today—but say it was a day like we had the other day . . . it was almost ninety. There's absolutely no shade for the dog. That would be a problem because the law says shelter or protection from the weather. It doesn't say just shelter." Although the officer agreed that the dog would likely be outside without shelter on future hot days, he chose to wait and say nothing to the respondent. "If I get another complaint or if I am in the area someday, I may swing by and see if the dog is out if it's really hot," he noted. They also were less aggressive than animal-inclined peers when they felt that human concerns took precedence over animal issues, especially if the latter were deemed not to be urgent or life-threatening. In one instance, an officer decided to back away from arguing with a crying respondent over how she was caring for her dog because the respondent's child also was there. He said: "In my mind, the most important thing was that child, and how that child must feel because her mother's crying. And so, I was trying to get the lady to calm down for the child's sake. Somebody else might say that the most important thing was the animal, but my feeling was that the dog was not suffering and he was not going to die."

Certainly, part of their retreat from being aggressive was a sentiment shared with regular police not to work too hard on cases. For example, studies have found that new officers quickly learn that hard work goes unrewarded and consequently avoid situations that might create trouble, such as making arrests (Petersilia et al. 1987). Colleagues who work harder than others are resented as "rate busters" (Van Maanen 1975), as police-oriented officers viewed their animal-inclined peers in the department. However, their criticism was not just based on the extra effort of animal-inclined officers but on their flagrant and dangerous use of emotions. This made police-oriented officers uneasy because it contradicted their detached presentation of self and brought humane law enforcement precariously close to being identified with the unchecked and unprofessional emotions of animal control work and animal activism.

A Mission

As opposed to their police-oriented peers, animal-inclined officers were more likely to be, but not exclusively, female and younger, and often identified themselves as pet owners, "animal people," or vegetarians. While a few sympathized with animal right activists and their cause, all professed a strong interest in having animals in their personal lives and holding them in high regard. Interest in animals colored how and where they lived, as well as the kind of friends they kept. One such officer recounted how his concern for animals affected decisions about whom to date:

> Yeah, I had a girlfriend a while back. I make a joke about this, but there is some truth to it. After the first couple of dates I had with the

woman, I would be like, "Here's a multiple choice question. We have tickets to *Phantom of the Opera*. We've waited months to see this, we've paid hundreds of dollars, and we are running late. We're in tuxedo and gown and we are flying down there. And we see an animal, a dog, a cat, a squirrel thrashing in the street that was just hit by a car. What do we do? A: do we keep driving? B: do we keep driving till we get to a telephone where we call someone that hopefully will respond and pick it up? Or C: pick it up, forget about the show and bring it to an animal hospital." Anything less than C, I don't see her again. Well, I never really asked her the question, but the answer came from a situation. It wasn't *Phantom of the Opera*, it was a ballet. There was a cat jumping around in the street. I stopped and said, "Sorry, we are going to the animal hospital." She broke up with me. She said that I was too . . . animals came first in my life and that she couldn't handle someone like that. I said, "Thank you. I'm glad I found out now because, yes, animals come first."

Animals clearly played a dominant role in their personal lives and they wanted to extend that concern into their jobs.

Their attraction to humane law enforcement stemmed from its goal of helping animals per se, as opposed to its police functions. Many had histories working for organizations that helped animals and they continued to do so after hours. Several worked in animal shelters before taking their current jobs or volunteered for these organizations now. One such officer, on his own time, raised funds and wrote a newsletter for an animal shelter, and "fostered" stray cats until homes could be found for them. Indeed, in one sense, the job disappointed many of them because it afforded few opportunities to have direct contact with animals, contacts that they particularly sought and valued. Whenever possible, they approached animals to interact with them when at work. One such officer, while driving to investigate a complaint, saw several dogs walking on the sidewalk. She pulled over, got out of the car, petted two of the dogs, gave them "treats" from a bag kept for this purpose in the rear of the vehicle, and laughed with amusement as a third dog climbed into the driver's seat. But for most, they prized their jobs as a special opportunity or mission to help animals, despite how little contact they had with them during the work day.

Their feeling for cruelty work went beyond a personal interest in animals; it symbolized an ideological passion about the job. Humane law enforcement continued their lifelong desire to address and remedy the plight of animals needing protection—it was a calling that made them feel uniquely suited for this job or for similar work. One officer clearly expressed this view: "If I ever gave up this job, what would I do? I couldn't show up at someone's door and make someone listen to me on how to take care of their pet or how they should treat their animals. That's where my heart and soul is. I couldn't logically see myself doing anything else and really be happy doing it because my life is so centered around the animals." These officers also could not imagine leaving the job because they considered themselves to be irreplaceable. Like others on a mission, no one could do their work as well as they could. If they quit, no one could replace their eagerness and ability to help animals. Speaking about this attitude, one officer said that as a child, "I would take in a stray dog and I would say to my mother, 'Do you know how many of these they kill every year?' And she goes, 'What are you going to do, get all of them?' And that's what I feel like. I always have that 'nobody can do this job as well as me' attitude. That's my mentality, like if I left this job, who is going to do it as well as I can?" And, if for some reason they left humane law enforcement, they expected to continue to work for animal welfare and protection. As one officer said with conviction, "I want to do as much as I can here and then I'll find another way of helping animals that I haven't explored yet."

As a mission, they found themselves personally involved in their cruelty work. Rather than detaching their emotions or separating work from the rest of their lives, as did police-oriented colleagues, these officers let their work "bother" or "get to" them. As one claimed, "I have a strange passion for animals. I'm not a normal person when it comes to animals. It makes it a lot harder when things bother you as opposed to writing a speeding ticket for somebody. There's nothing emotional about that." Because they became emotionally involved in their work, these officers "took their work home" and worried about their cases. An officer described one such instance where he wondered what happened to the animal in question, a white, fluffy medium-sized dog considered to be "real friendly" with a muzzle embedded in his mouth. "He was cut and scraped. The muzzle was way too tight and it never came off. I told them to leave the muzzle off until its face heals, but there's nothing illegal about putting a muzzle on. As soon as that dog's face heals up, they can put the muzzle back. How do I know they didn't just say,

'Yeah, whatever,' and when I left, put the muzzle back on and the dog is still sitting there.'"

Though their work troubled them, these officers expected to feel this way and considered angst to be part of the job itself. Many situations where animals were not abused according to the law bothered them in addition to more tragic, egregious cases. For example, some were saddened to see dogs tied to their outdoor shelters, especially if they had few human contacts: "That's something that will always bother me," said one officer. Others were moved by abused animals

that continued to show affection to people, as the following officer elaborated: "When you go up and you've got a horse snuggling on you or the dog is jumping up, you go, 'Look what someone's doing to you,' and they still love you no matter what. That gets to me." Nor did their emotions trail off with more experience. Some spoke about how the job still "got" to them even after

Despite an attempt to drown it, this dog was still able to show affection to its rescuers.

years of case work. One said, "The first few years of this job, you really have to play a lot of head games with yourself and get over it. Sometimes I think I'm dealing with this job a little bit better. Then I'm like, I've been doing it for ten years! You hope that eventually you can deal with it." In short, they dealt with cruelty by allowing themselves to be disturbed by it on and off the job, and by seeing these emotions as a legitimate expression of concern by professionals involved in this kind of work.

Cases frequently disturbed animal-inclined officers because they applied their own personal standards of humane care and found respondents' care to be lacking even though they were not violating the law. That it would be lacking was inevitable because officers saw respondent's animals as though they were their own, and expected them to be treated as well as they would treat them. This attitude was evident in the words of one officer who claimed that the animals "all become mine. They're all mine. Even if I haven't seen it, it's still mine. I don't care if the owner is sitting there, that's my dog, you know. It's always been like that.

Every animal that I talk to is automatically mine." A fellow officer had a similar sentiment: "That's what bothers me, that I can't make them look at their dog the way I look at my dog and my cat that are side by side on my bed when I leave in the morning and have a bowl of water. Every time I give them a bowl of water, it just blows my mind that there are dogs that are begging for water. And that's why I'll probably never get satisfaction from this job."

Applying personal standards of care happened most often when animals were treated like property. In one case, a dog appeared to be completely ignored by the respondent, leading the officer to comment: "I feel bad because they [dogs] just want company and they just want to be loved and played with." In another instance, the officer was bothered by a situation where there were no neglect or cruelty violations, but the respondent seemed uninterested in his dog, which was tied up in the backyard, serving merely to guard the house. As the officer spoke to this respondent, the dog persistently tried to reach the officer and the respondent, apparently to play or greet them, but could not because he was limited by a chain. After leaving the house, the officer confided that it disturbed her to see the dog ignored, being kept only to scare intruders. She noted, "A dog like that is probably one of the saddest things I see in my work. It's not a way to keep a dog. Why have one? The dog is going to spend its entire existence on that chain running back and forth, getting a ball so somebody will play with it. That's the sweetest dog. That dog wouldn't bite you in a million years." Although seeing this disturbed the officer, she did not say anything to the respondent about the dog's lowly status as property, since there were no cruelty violations.

Applying personal standards of humane care, officers' expectations sometimes smacked of rescue fantasies that far exceeded what the law required. One such officer talked about wanting to "save" all animals, even if it meant that she would not eat: "If you're going to own a pet, you do everything for it. I don't care if you don't eat for a week. I can't go out and enforce that because I know that's not the way everybody else thinks and that's not the law. I know I can't save everyone, but I can do my best at saving the ones that I can." Another animal-inclined officer investigated a no-shelter case and found that the respondent had a kitten which the officer wanted to protect. Her urge was to get the cat out of its present situation and into a safe place, even though the respondent did nothing to violate the cruelty code. She noted, "I have a tough time with some cases. I was at a house this morning and there's this little kitten walking around my feet and no one's answering the door. I just wanted to scoop up that kitten and get it out of there so it doesn't get run over or so I know it's okay." And yet another officer was concerned that dogs might not be kept warm enough during the winter if kept in "igloo" shelters. She fantasized about using a temperature probe to see if these small shelters really worked. "There's so many things that you would like to do," she said. "I think about them all the time."

Their emotional involvement in cases meant that animal-inclined officers sometimes showed strong feelings when meeting respondents who seemed neglectful or cruel. As one officer said, "I've seen stuff that's really bad and you just go, 'You've got to be shitting me. Look at this dog. You are a piece of shit!'" Another officer elaborated this sentiment: "I feel horrible for the animals, and I get

This dog has been left to starve to death. Officers must use their anger at such abuse in constructive ways.

very, very angry. Me just sitting there feeling bad for the animal doesn't help his situation. If I get mad, then that makes my mind work. I don't mean mad like I'm going to go out and punch them, but I mean mad, like what can I do to these people to get this dog out of there or to get them to improve the situation." Especially with rookies, anger sometimes spilled over into encounters with respondents. One officer talked about how he handled cases: "I'm preachy and I'm critical of people. I mean, I'm working on toning that down. Like, I'll go over and the dog will have no shelter and I'll go, 'The dog needs to have shelter.' And I'll get one of those blank stares, 'It does?' 'Well, would you like that?' 'But it's a dog.' And that kind of gets you going a little bit. I may sound condescending to people, but I'm brand new, cut me a little bit of slack."

Animal-inclined officers criticized police-oriented peers because their strict reading and enforcement of the law stopped them from intervening. They felt they needed to be more aggressive when investigating cases, as one of the former officers illustrated, "I think Officer Dan is laid back. Sometimes he'll spend too much time giving the people the benefit of the doubt and not really get tough on them quick enough. That doesn't work for me. I get really emotionally involved." Another animal-inclined officer said of a colleague: "Like Officer Bernie, I think he's an excellent police officer. But he has no emotion. I think he goes out there and if he doesn't see a blatant violation, I don't think he's going to say anything." Animal-inclined officers believed that the less aggressive approach jeopardized the well-being of animals. One officer criticized a colleague because of inaction on a case involving a drug-addicted respondent who allegedly failed to care for his dog, including feeding it raw chicken to make it vicious, along with frequent beatings:

> Officer Artie comes back and goes, "He's got a plastic container under the house that the dog can crawl in for shelter and it really wasn't much, but he was really strung out on crack." That meant to me to get that dog out, regardless. Well, the dog was very thin, and he talked to him. He went there with "no shelter and thin." Well, "yeah, I feed it raw chicken." Well there's no law against that, if it keeps him healthy, which eventually it won't, but . . . so when I came back, he told me that, and I just shook my head. I went over there and put the guy through the ringer and the guy gave me the dog. Its primary diet was raw chicken and orange juice. So that right there indicates a health problem, okay. The dog had never seen a veterinarian, it was way un- derweight, and the shelter was not adequate. But Officer Artie didn't find the same violations that we would. Granted, it might have even been pushing it. If he had turned the container around so the opening wasn't facing out into the elements so the dog could crawl in from be- hind it and get in, well then, that might be adequate shelter under the state's definition. But we are not required to tell him how to fix the situation.

Another example of jeopardizing animals happened when respondents consid- ered abandoning them on the streets. Animal-inclined officers picked up these unwanted animals when police-oriented officers did not. "They [police-oriented officers] leave it up to the owner, if they don't want the dog. If someone says to me, 'I really can't keep the dog, do you want it?' 'Yep.' I'll take it because they may turn it out. If they're going to give it to me and I know that it's not the best situation for the dog, I'm going to take it and throw it in the car."

By contrast, animal-inclined staff tried to provide "humane" solutions to problems at hand. One officer described this approach: "Some officers have a very high level of sensitivity. They might go beyond what, you know, the law will allow you to do. They will try and do things for people that aren't within the laws—you should do this, that, and the other thing. It wasn't a violation of the law; they just felt that they wanted to do this. Other officers will go [beyond] that." An officer used the example of an animal hoarder to compare her method of investigation to that of a police-oriented colleague. She said: "When I go into a house and there's thirty cats, they're going to get euthanized. But I'd rather see them euthanized than suffering and then going hungry. And Officer Mat and I differ greatly on that. He would let them live in minimal circumstances. To me, I'd be inhumane if I left those cats there. I'd rather see them safe up in heaven playing with my dog." Another animal-inclined officer compared his handling of a fictitious case to how a police-oriented peer would do it. The case involved a dog constantly kept in a crate, but who was properly cleaned, fed, and watered. It was technically legal to do this, and the officer could picture his police-oriented peer saying there was no violation. "If I went there, I'd talk to them about how their muscles will just turn to nothing and how the animal's life isn't good because he can't move around. He's going to be prone to illness, which will cost them money. I'll try to appeal to their feelings more than the law."

Camps and Correctness

Although two camps existed in the department, differences among officers were not always clear-cut and mutually agreed upon. Several officers, pigeonholed by their colleagues into one camp, did not see themselves the same way. In one case, for instance, an officer seen by most of his colleagues as more police-oriented than animal-inclined did not see himself belonging to the former camp. As he described himself, "I don't like police work. I don't like that part of it. The only part of the job that I enjoy is helping animals and working with animals, but as far as the police powers go, that's another side of it. I'm not really interested in that kind of work. Even when we get to a point where they want to do a big investigation, that's not me. Give it to somebody else who wants to dig and dig and dig and follow people around. I would rather not do that part of it." For this officer, "police work" meant having an interest in "arresting somebody, getting involved with hoodlums, and doing undercover work, which I am uncomfortable with. Like I say, I'll climb trees, I'll go under buildings to help an animal, but as far as being Joe police officer—going to arrest this one and that one—I really don't care about that side of it." He saw himself more in the middle of the department, falling between those officers having a strong police emphasis and those having a "radical" emphasis.

These camps became caricatures of departmental extremes rather than accurate depictions of most officers' realities. For example, although animal-inclined officers did have strong personal beliefs about how animals should be cared for, these beliefs did not influence their case management to the degree thought by police-oriented officers. And for their part, police-oriented officers brought more sentiment and personal opinion to their investigations than suggested by their image and assumed by animal-inclined colleagues.

Nevertheless, many officers treated these camps as real, placed themselves and their colleagues into one of them, and had an opinion about their relative appropriateness. The existence of these camps is not surprising. Individuals whose work is defined by some abstract principle or standard of behavior often compete with each other to see who can best achieve these ends. This competition is aggravated in situations where the primary mission or goal of the group is vague, as is the case with combating animal cruelty. These camps also should not surprise us because our general culture is divided on how humans should relate to animals, seeing them either as utilitarian objects to be used or as valued companions. Humane law enforcement officers capture this dualism as police-oriented members carry out their work "objectively," detached from the plight of animals, while animal-inclined members carry out their work passionately, emotionally affected by their cases. The former make a distinction between the moral worth of humans versus that of animals, while the latter do not.

These camps created a sense of "humane correctness" within the department. This correctness involved a number of issues—including, but not limited to, rodeos, hunting, and vegetarianism—that were sensitive and important issues in the department as well as in the humane society. As a form of correctness, officers' thoughts and feelings about these issues, depending on where they stood, conveyed moral statements about their character. One officer, for example, felt that she was not humanely correct because she liked rodeos and was not a vegetarian, among other things. "When I'm working, if someone asks me on the street what I think, I'm representing the MSPCA, so I have to give them the MSPCA view, 'rodeos are bad.' But, personally, I would go if I had the time. Officer Randy [animal-inclined] knows it and he's like, 'Oh, you!' And I'm seeing this guy who hunts and traps. And people are like, 'How could you go out with someone like that?'" Other officers did not see her as an "animal rights" person and claimed to have a different reaction to events such as rodeos. As one of these officers said, "I can't say that Officer Lynn doesn't care about animals, because she must. But she certainly isn't on the same level of protectionism as myself or even Officer Ginny. I would consider us closer to animal rights than anything else. Officer Lynn loves the rodeo. If I go to the rodeo, the only thing I want is to put handcuffs on every-one in sight and help those animals from the legalized torture they are enduring." Another officer also fell short of the department's stance on humane correctness because he did not oppose ox pulls or pet stores and condemn those who partici-pated in these activities or owned these stores. He said: "I don't think that because a guy pulls an ox, uses oxen, that they're bad people because they do that. We have some officers that think that. If a guy owns a pet store and the guy is pulling horses or oxen, he's a jerk or he's a bad person. And I don't categorize people that way. That's their party. If they choose to do it, and they do it in a responsible manner, I don't think they're a bad person."

These camps caused problems other than the disagreement over humane correctness. The existence of twin expectations frustrated some officers because they could not equally emphasize or give expression both to police and animal concerns. Failing to live up to one of these orientations made some officers feel as though they were neither "regular" police nor "advocates" for animals. Yet, such problems were a small price to pay for the organizational value of having two ori-entations. This division made it possible for individual officers to take on occupa-tional identities appropriate for them, while connecting the department in the public's eye both to police and animal work.

Distancing

Humane officers also dealt with their precarious occupational identity by distanc-ing themselves from animal control. While there was some tension within the department between the police and animal camps, almost all officers complained about or denigrated animal control workers. Of course, most officers praised the work of at least a few animal control workers who were seen as helpful. For exam-ple, officers liked it when the latter took over classic "dogcatcher" cases, rather than referring them to humane law enforcement. In fact, most felt that animal control workers should handle more "no-shelter" complaints and fewer "cruelty" cases. As one officer said, "If it's a cruelty case, you don't really want animal control dealing with it. Not that they aren't smart enough or anything. If they don't deal with cruelty a lot, and just do leash law violations and stuff like that, they're not really going to know how to deal with the cruelty cases. So you don't really want them to. But a shelter call, that's ridiculous. They could go out there."

Despite the rare praise, humane law enforcement officers typically put animal control workers below them in the general law enforcement pecking order. Or, as one officer said of them: "Animal control . . . it's a lower . . . I like to look at us as a higher standard. We go to the academy. We do all this other stuff. We do more search warrants than your average cop does. And we prosecute all our stuff in court, while the average cop has the police prosecutors." This boundary work enabled humane officers to construct and clarify their identities and occupational margins. Like the boundary work of other occupations whose jurisdictions were ambiguous and claimed by competing groups (Allen 2000), humane officers relied on micro-political strategies to demarcate a division of labor. Their primary strategy was casual chatter that served as a powerful symbolic device to make this demarcation, at least among themselves. While the specific details of their talk about animal control could at times seem petty to outsiders, the larger message underlying it was not trivial.

Humane officers disparaged animal control in several ways. First, many were thought to be unprofessional. For example, some officers criticized their appearance. As one observed, "Like South Town, I know the animal control person there. She picks up dead skunks and stuff like that, but she doesn't wear a uniform and she kind of wears sweats. She doesn't look very professional and she's even said, 'How do we get people to take me more seriously?'" Others claimed that some were unprofessional because they simply did not "care" about helping animals. One humane officer said that when he contacted them for help, they rarely did anything. Explaining his disappointing experience, he said: "They don't care. Some are police doing it on the side. Some are just people who like animals and realize that they get paid six thousand dollars and they are on call twenty-four hours and they hate it. Some are dog officers, not in their job description—it's just how they view themselves. So don't call a dog officer about a skunk or a raccoon or a cat or anything. They will just say, 'No, I don't deal with that.'" Another officer cited the case of barking dogs to show how animal control officers did not care about correcting animal-related problems, instead creating bureaucratic excuses to not work: "A lot of animal control officers will not respond to a barking dog complaint unless someone makes a complaint in writing. Say for instance the city of Westminster—if you want them to investigate or do anything about a barking dog, they require a complaint in writing." And others felt that their inaccessibility made them unprofessional. Many had other jobs, making it hard to reach them or, if contacted, making them available only after normal work hours. As one officer pointed out, "Like this town here, if we had a problem—a dog that got hit by a car or something—I don't think we would be able to get the animal control officer because it's probably a situation that the guy works at the mill during the day and he's an ACO when he's off weekends, that kind of thing." "It's not professional at all. They go out when they feel like it," decried one officer. In another instance, an officer claimed that a dog had been running loose for two days and animal control, although it had been called days earlier, did not get the dog. He noted, "I know that they get sick of dealing with some of these people too, but it's inexcusable for animal control to not show up in a two-day period."

Second, animal control workers were thought to be inadequately trained. Speaking for her geographical area, one humane officer claimed: "Most animal control officers down here are absolutely clueless even as to the difference between a poodle and a pit bull." Another officer related an example of this sort of poor job preparation. It involved a case where the animal control worker wanted to seize a horse because she considered it to be severely neglected, starved, and in need in emergency veterinary care. "When I got down there, I saw the horse. I didn't see a problem. So I said to her, 'Why did you do this?' She said, 'Well, I thought the horse was bad enough that it should have been taken.' I said, 'No, this horse is not bad. Yeah, he's a little bit down on weight, but it's nothing I'm concerned over.' She doesn't know. They tend to be hired with no expertise and no training, and they are given a badge." This inadequate training, according to officers, led to incompetence on the job. In one case, an animal control worker investigated a dog that allegedly killed chickens. She confiscated the dog, kept it for twelve hours, and then shot it. Cruelty charges were brought against her because it was only legal to shoot animals caught in the act of bothering livestock. An officer described the owner's shock and reaction to this ineptly handled case. "So she calls animal control, 'You picked my dog up this morning and I'd like it back.' She says, 'Well, you can have your dog back, but he won't be wagging his tail because he's dead. But if you'd like me to bring the carcass over, I'd be more than happy to do that.' The lady wasn't home and she placed it on the lawn next to her clothes line. The lady came back from work and there was her dog." The owner sued the town's animal control department.

Third, animal control workers incorrectly referred cases to humane law enforcement, claimed officers. Of course, not all referrals were considered to be inappropriate. Because humane officers had greater authority, animal control workers sometimes asked them for help with difficult respondents. Some respondents, claimed an officer, "will ignore animal control. They will be jerks. So animal control won't be able to get anything done." Another officer described an "unsanitary conditions" complaint first handled by an animal control worker who tried to correct the situation until she failed and called humane law enforcement to step in, take charge, and obtain compliance: "She told her [respondent] what to do. When she went back and checked again, it still hadn't been done, so she called us. We have more authority, and we tell them about the laws and the fines, and they wake up. When I went in, it wasn't sanitary. I read her the riot act. She had two dog houses that looked like they'd been in a world war. I said, 'You gotta do something. You can't keep this dog out here with this shelter.'" Nevertheless, some of their referrals should not have been made, claimed officers, who assumed that animal control workers' frustration led them to refer these cases to humane law enforcement instead of grappling with them. As an officer said about one case where she suspected this: "Animal control probably got sick of answering her [complainant] calls and said, 'Give it to the MSPCA.' And that ticks me off. They could call me personally and say something to me like, 'Gee, we're having a problem with this lady . . . '"

Fourth, other officers claimed that animal control workers could become overzealous when helping animals. However, not all zealousness was criticized by officers. At times, officers understood and lauded the efforts of animal control workers. For example, one applauded an animal control worker who had a passionate commitment to finding homes for unwanted animals. She noted, "The one in Mill Town, she's really into her job. She's got like five dogs at home that she couldn't find homes for and she didn't want to be put to sleep so she took them home. She's got animals in the pound that have been there for like a year that she says, 'One day, someone will come and adopt them.' That kind of thing." More commonly, officers questioned their zealousness. In some cases, they thought that animal control workers sensed "something isn't right" and expected respondents to behave accordingly, even though it was not a violation of law. In other cases, officers felt that animal control workers "panicked" and inappropriately magnified cruelty violations. One officer described the problem of "exaggerating" complaints. She said: "They'll say, 'My God, it's terrible.' And we get there and it's okay. It's a violation, but really not too bad. Some can be almost fanatical about complaints. I have compassion, but I try to be objective. They tend to panic. Like a 'dog messing in the yard, very foul odor,' they'll call it in and exaggerate the complaint, like 'Oh, it's extremely unsanitary. The dog can't get out of its own mess. There is a terrible odor.'"

Officers empathized with the personal beliefs of animal control workers, but objected to them enforcing their beliefs. One said: "You get the ones that call and want to do something about something that they think isn't right. And I might not think it's right either, but we have to remember, we've got laws we have to work with. You have to be careful what you tell people. You don't say, 'Do it or else,' especially if you are not within the law," said an officer. For example, one animal control worker threatened to illegally take some cats that appeared to be neglected but not to the extent of being in violation of the cruelty code, according to an officer: "She said, 'I think I'll break into the apartment and steal the cats.' She can't do that. She told me that's she would go to jail to get these poor cats a home. I said, 'You can't think that way.' You see a lot of animal control officers, they get too emotional and just want to break in and take the animal and end the complaint. I believe that some people don't deserve to have animals. I would love to say, 'You don't deserve to have an animal' and take it, but you can't." In another case, an animal control worker trespassed into a respondent's backyard by climbing over a tall wooden fence that concealed her view. The officer present criticized this blatant trespassing, but also appreciated her help with the case and acknowledged the limitation of his own more conservative approach to such situations. He said: "You can't do that. I feel better because she's been coming here for rechecks and everything, but I wouldn't do that. What I would do is leave a card on the outside, have them call me, and make an appointment to see the dog. The downside is they can clean everything up before I get there."

Of course, officers did not consciously distance themselves from animal control to establish their primacy in the law enforcement division of labor. They had genuine concerns about animal control. Yet, by pointing out their lack of professionalism and competence, the put-downs, snide remarks, and gossip of officers accomplished something larger. It was in their very willingness to critique animal control, no matter how petty the complaint or how many exceptions existed, that a rhetorical leitmotif circulated in the department making every officer, and those with whom they spoke, aware of the margins between animal control and animal police. In their criticisms, officers implied that they possessed the worthy traits absent in most animal control workers. Nor was it ironic that their criticisms of animal control mirrored how they were criticized by regular police and others. Issues of professionalism and competence are at the symbolic core of all divisions of labor and will be negotiated as groups jostle for occupational position. In the end, such distancing clarified the occupational identity of animal police for officers themselves as well as for the public and professionals.

◆ ◆ ◆

Officers received a variety of messages about their work from different audiences. Few outsiders applauded their efforts to help animals; more were apt to confuse them with lower-status occupations. In particular, the link with animal control created a kind of occupational courtesy stigma for humane law enforcement. According to Goffman (1963), individuals with close ties to stigmatized others can themselves be seen this way. The mere connection contaminates them in the public's eye because they are intertwined and assumed to be similar. When animal police are victims of courtesy stigma, their status will be tarnished, if not lowered, because they are confused with the low-status work of animal control (Palmer 1978). The fact that they do not do "real police work" hurt their public image. If they were seen as legitimate police, it might negate the link with animal control, if not elevate their standing. Rather than suffering a courtesy stigma, they would enjoy the privileges of piggybacking a higher-status occupation. But this despite their efforts to cut the link to animal control, did not happen. In Hughes' terms (1972), they had the license to police for cruelty without the mandate to do so. Without such a mandate, their courtesy stigma thwarted the personal and professional goals of officers to protect animals and do police work.

Humane officers resisted the status-lowering connection to animal control workers as well as to animal rights activists. They did this by trying to affirm and clarify an occupational pecking order that positioned humane law enforcement squarely between regular police and animal control, while completely disconnecting themselves from animal rights. This division of labor enabled officers to approximate regular police as near colleagues and to distance animal control workers as virtual subordinates. Maintaining this central position required skillful role play by officers. Featuring the police side of their work carried the risk of being seen as insufficiently humane. Emphasizing the animal side of their job carried the risk of being seen as "not real cops."

Their response to this dilemma was novel and largely successful. On the one hand, individual officers could entertain either perspective, so the department as a whole represented both approaches. Most of the time, the two appeared to table their differences and carry on. Despite the dominance of the police-oriented perspective among officers, the rival animal inclination provided an important counterbalance, if not tension, within the department, making for muted disagreement. On the other hand, this tension surfaced when the two groups rubbed up against each other and found they could not tolerate the other's style, similar to the way that conflict sometimes emerges between divisions of regular police departments (Van Maanen 1992). Although neither group pressed things too far when this occurred, the tension reminded officers that they needed to respect the other camp's style by restraining their own. This recognition served as an informal governor within the department that kept in check the perspectives. Thus, the twin identities monitored each other and put a break on either "going too far" with their style of policing, much like other pluralist organizations having coalitions at the same hierarchical level that hold each other in check (Morgan 1981).

Ironically, cruelty officers' being at the center of a division of labor that merged regular police with animal control no doubt perpetuated the public's confusion about the nature of humane law enforcement. Merging the worlds of regular police with animal work created a hybrid identity understood by officers but not necessarily by outsiders. For the most part, the latter had no idea that certain police were officially entrusted with the job of managing animal cruelty. This confusion was most evident in the calls that came into the department. Officers and dispatchers tried to make sense of cruelty complaints by giving voice to or discounting the appeals of those reporting them, as we see next.

2

The Cruelty-Finding Exercise

> When you first get here, it is like a cop on a gun run. A cop, when he gets a call for a gun immediately thinks there's a guy with a gun out there that's going to do harm to somebody. When you get a job here that says "dog out with no food, water, or shelter" you kind of get jaded after a while because when you first go out there, you are like [excited, enthused voice] "oh, there's a dog out [there] without food, water, or shelter! It must be dying!"

Every day, humane law enforcement departments are flooded with hundreds of telephone calls suspecting or alleging cruelty. These citizen callers, much like those who contact regular police departments (Antunes and Scott 1981; Black 1980), want to initiate action by officers. To manage this flood and screen calls for their appropriateness, telephone dispatchers act as gatekeepers. They decide which calls should be stamped, numbered, and recorded as cruelty complaints and subsequently be investigated by officers. New dispatchers assume that it will be easy to sort incoming calls into those that potentially involve cruelty, and therefore need to be checked by humane officers, and those that do not. For their part, officers investigate complaints given them by dispatchers, deciding which ones qualify as cruelty under the law and which ones merit intervention or prosecution. New officers assume that it will be easy to figure out which cases represent clear-cut animal cruelty, and they believe their interventions can prevent further harm to animals by changing the abuser's behavior or by punishing them in court.

The expectations of rookie dispatchers and officers are disappointed as they acquire on-the-job experience. Dispatchers find themselves overwhelmed by calls that fall short of their original expectation of handling incidents of egregious animal cruelty. Instead, they find themselves searching for potential cruelty in the allegations of callers who, more often than not, describe prosaic animal problems. In turn, this stretching of calls into cruelty complaints makes officers feel overwhelmed with cases that are a far cry from the kind of cruelty they expected to investigate as rookies. Rather than being overly generous with their working definition of cruelty, as the dispatchers are, officers reject many of the complaints they get because in their eyes they are not legitimate animal cruelty cases.

Although the ambiguity of complainants' reports causes dispatchers and officers to wrestle with the meaning of cruelty, it is also due to the ambiguity of the anti-cruelty law. Despite legislative efforts to make the law as specific as possible, its clarity falls woefully short when department members have to apply it. The reality faced by dispatchers and officers is hardly as black and white as the wording of the law first appears. They discover its shortcomings and find it difficult to apply, leaving them quite a bit of discretion to determine which animals become bona fide cruelty victims deserving help. Like the discretion of regular police who operate as "street-level bureaucrats" (Wilson 1973, 8), animal police and dispatchers are forced to create a working definition of cruelty by interpreting and applying the law on a case by case basis. Understanding how complaints get processed shows what cruelty means "on the streets" rather than in the abstractions of codes and laws.

Stretching

Most dispatchers were drawn to the job because they cared about animals and wanted to protect them. Although they

---

$200.00 REWARD

Offered by the MSPCA for information leading to the identity and conviction of the person(s) responsible for the death and mutilation of the cat pictured below. This crime occured in the Roslindale area during May 1985.

All information should be sent to the MSPCA Law Enforcement Division

Such reward posters help alert the public to the presence of animal cruelty and the need for officers to combat it.

did not work directly with victimized animals, newcomers expected to play an important role in fighting cruelty by identifying likely cases and mobilizing resources to stop abuse and neglect. One dispatcher recalled why she took the job: "I saw an ad in the paper that said, 'Animal lover needed. Be a front-line warrior in the crusade against cruelty to animals.' " Another thought about joining the department after seeing a reward poster.

However, new dispatchers found most calls were not what they expected. Few represented extreme cruelty while most involved animals without shelter, food, water, or medical care. Moreover, many of the latter were difficult to classify as cruelty under the law's provisions. What gets categorized as "cruelty" were reports of undernourished, unsheltered, and untreated animals—a far cry from the expectations of novice dispatchers who wanted to wage a "crusade against cruelty." Short of weather-related, no-shelter emergencies, the vast majority of these calls were seen as "only" no-shelter complaints. One dispatcher illustrated this blasé attitude in a hypothetical conversation with an officer: "When an officer calls in and he'll say, 'Do I have any complaints?' I'll say, 'Yeah, you have one complaint. It's just a no-shelter. It can wait until tomorrow, depending on the weather.'"

Often a complaint about an inadequate shelter falls short of the rookie's idea of cruelty.

Dispatchers became humanely desensitized, although not indifferent, to shelter-related complaints because the constant volume of calls wore them down and made it hard for them to picture the plight of these animals. "Like everything, you just get used to it. It's not horrifying," observed one dispatcher. Another compared seeing a no-shelter case to hearing about one: "You get kind of used to it. If I were to drive by a house and see a dog sitting in a pile of snow, without water, looking thin, that would make me angry and pull at my heart strings. But when you deal with them over the phone and every other call is a no shelter, you begin to think of it as a 'no shelter' and you don't picture the animal in your head anymore. The other calls that you don't get regularly, they tug at you more because you are not used to hearing them constantly." The ceaseless flood of no-shelter reports blunted their emotional reactions to these calls. Sheer repetition, combined with the second-hand nature of the complaints, minimized the vividness and novelty of what callers described. Organizational routine replaced the moral outrage of rookie dispatchers.

Dispatchers' humane sensitivity also was lessened because they felt that some officers did little to curtail animal neglect and cruelty. From their perspective, cases may not be vigorously investigated by officers who appeared indifferent to complaints. One former dispatcher explained: "After you are here for four years—that's a long time to be in the dispatcher's job—I saw what it did to Jane [former dispatcher]. She's rebounding though. She'll be back to human soon. You have to know that this job's going to drive you crazy. A few of our officers . . . not all of them . . . but there are a couple who would rather cut out early than go out on a call. When they do that, it makes you unhappy and angry and unfulfilled."

Yet, most dispatchers maintained their humane sensitivity by adopting the perspectives of callers and animals. They did this by trying to regard most complaints as "important," or as one dispatcher said: "It's something we feel the officer should go and see because it seemed important enough. You know there's an animal out there." Even routine reports of animals without shelters could disturb dispatchers who had the following reaction: "In any of these calls, animals can be caused discomfort. If an animal is being left outside with no shelter, that hurts if you are outside in the middle of the winter. I don't want to sound melodramatic, but every one of them is serious. There is no trivial animal abuse." It was evident that dispatchers genuinely cared about the fate of animals in these cases. For one, they sometimes checked with officers after they investigated cases to see how animals fared. "I may want to find out what happened. If there's someone I dealt with on the phone with a serious situation, the next time the officer calls in, I'll ask him about it. Just for my own curiosity, I may ask," explained one dispatcher.

To treat complaints as important and get them investigated, dispatchers and callers "stretched" incoming calls because they fell short of the legal definition of cruelty. Dispatchers claimed that callers exaggerated their reports because "they feel the need to do that to make it sound like it's legitimate and it needs investigating. I think people feel if they don't make it sound ugly enough, then we're not going to do anything." Obviously, callers did not think that dispatchers might help them stretch their complaints into investigations. As they did their own stretching, callers created personal definitions of cruelty that were different from formal definitions that presumably guided the work of dispatchers. "In some cases, I think it's something that fits their definition of cruelty. They see something they don't like and make a complaint," observed one dispatcher.

New dispatchers unwittingly participated in stretching because they tended to believe callers' reports and write them up as cruelty complaints. One dispatcher described how on-the-job experience led her to doubt the accuracy of these reports: "I found that most people exaggerate and that completely surprised me. When I first started working here, I'd take a complaint and I'd be listening to them thinking everything they said was true and just being horrified. And then, time after time, you have the officer come back and say, 'No, that's not what I found. It wasn't anything like that.' It really shocks me that about 90 percent of the calls we get are exaggerated."

Not so unwittingly, more seasoned dispatchers also stretched many reports. Because they assumed that animals needed visits by officers, even if callers sounded like they "were blowing in the wind," experienced dispatchers adopted a generous and open attitude when they processed these complaints. One described this approach when taking complaints over the telephone. After going through a list of questions with callers, her last comment was to ask, "'If you think the animal's life is in danger or it's not cared for properly, then we will send someone.' And they'll say, 'I'd feel better if you people looked.' So you take the complaint because you don't know until you get there. And you might get the one that you think, just by the telephone conversation, 'Oh, these people are blowing wind, there's nothing there,' and you get there and it's disgusting. And you say, 'Gee, they were right.'" The following dispatcher compared a report by a caller that is easily turned down to one that could be stretched: "Things like barking, loose dogs. A lot of people feel that letting dogs run loose all the time is cruelty. Well, technically it isn't. It's just a violation of leash law, so therefore it's an animal control issue. But if they say things that could be stretched to the dog's not getting proper care, but it isn't definitely a clear issue of cruelty to animals, I might take it."

The most common example of stretching involved callers who believed that barking dogs were suffering because of cruel treatment. "Barking—it's not something we enforce, so it's not something that we are going to deal with. But a lot of people will say 'the dog is barking—he's unhappy, he's howling, he's crying—that's not cruelty.' If they can see the dog and they can see the dog is physically fine, it's not cruelty. We can't really take that. I mean they say 'the dog is howling, he's screaming, he sounds in pain.'" Although these complaints rarely met the legal criteria for cruelty, dispatchers preferred to err on the safe side and investigate them just in case animals were at risk. As one dispatcher explained: "If certain officers are in the area, they might swing by, if not, I might call animal control or ask them [caller] to, and follow up the next day. But probably if it's just a barking dog—especially if it's a beagle because they have that really high-pitched bark—it's probably just a barking dog. But I can't assume that. If there's a possibility the animal is in danger, it's my obligation to dispatch an officer out there. If they want to get angry that they went out for nothing, then that's a different situation."

Of course, dispatchers did not automatically initiate investigations simply because dogs were purportedly loose or barking. They listened for more specific indications of cruelty that allowed them to proceed with complaints and to start investigations. For example, one dispatcher spoke about how she listened for "key words" that signaled cruelty in a complaint: "You know, she's saying, 'I hate my

neighbor. I've had a feud with my neighbor for ten years. The dog barks all night. I can't sleep.' And I'm like, 'Nope.' But then at the end, she says those key words, 'The dog's really thin.' I'll take it even though I think she might be herself stretching it to find something to get us out there. I have to take it. And I've told officers, 'It sounds like there are a lot of underlying things going on, but she claims thin dog.'" In addition to listening for key words, dispatchers tried to tease out sufficient information from callers to warrant investigations. As one said, "Someone calls and they are very concerned, but all of their concerns really are more just emotional. And you don't want to be like, 'Gee, your concerns are totally invalid.' You want to be like, 'I hear what you're saying, but we're going to have to come up with a little bit more to get us to be able to look at it and justify us looking into it.'" For example, one dispatcher talked about how she gathered information to stretch a "dog looks horrible" call: "We get a lot of 'The dog just looks horrible.' Well, I can't write, 'Dog looks horrible.' 'What do you mean,

A complaint about a "thin dog" led officers to this emaciated animal. Dispatchers have to judge whether a complaint warrants an investigation.

is he very skinny? Does he show signs of illness or something? What exactly does horrible mean?' Or we get a lot of 'They never feed him.' 'Well, when you say they don't feed him, how does the dog look to you?' 'Oh, no, he looks okay.' 'Then what makes you think they don't feed him?'"

Other calls were even harder to stretch into investigations, but dispatchers did so under certain circumstances. These "borderline" situations were often thought to merit some intervention because animals needed help. As one dispatcher said of this distinction, "If it's a straight out animal cruelty thing, then I will take it as a complaint and I'll stamp it. If it's borderline and I just think they might be able to do something that's going to improve the situation, then I'll ask them [officers] and see what they can do." A number of borderline situations existed.

Some were "emergencies" where animals might suffer, but were not victims of cruelty per se. In these circumstances, dispatchers often requested officers to intervene if animal control could not. "It's hard because only certain things are cruelty. I mean, an animal hit by a car is clearly an emergency, but it's not necessarily cruelty. It's going to be an animal control issue, but if somehow we have an officer in the area and animal control is not around, we'll have an officer go out there and see what they can do," said one dispatcher. Subjective factors, such as "tone of voice," helped them evaluate the urgency of an animal's situation, although these factors were unreliable and sometimes resulted in pointless visits by officers. In the words of one dispatcher, "The person's tone of voice plays into it, but you can't go just by that because you never know the type of people that are calling. A lot of times I'll tell an officer that it sounds like an emergency and he'll get out there and it's not . . . but if it sounds like an emergency, as far as I'm concerned, it is. And if he gets out there and sees differently, then okay, but at least he got out there."

Abandoned animals were common "emergencies" that got stretched, even though these unfortunate situations usually did not qualify as cruelty under the law. Classifying these cases as cruelty was difficult because respondents could lie about the disappearance of their animals. For example, sometimes people moved out of their homes and left behind dogs, technically roaming free. It was then hard to charge them with abandonment because they could claim that the dogs ran away and say they were looking for them without success. "It's a really easy way to get away with it," said one dispatcher. Another reason why it was difficult to classify these cases as cruelty had to do with the nuances of the law that made it possible for respondents to legally abandon their animals under certain conditions. For instance, neighbors occasionally called dispatchers to say that a respondent moved into a building that did not allow pets, but was coming back every day to feed the animal in the empty house. "He's got a dog house there and the owner is coming back and feeding him on a daily basis, but they've left him on the property because they can't take him with them. They figure nobody cares. Nobody will notice. Technically, you can do that. As long as you're coming back and feeding him. It's not going to be abandonment."

Dispatchers were troubled by the plight of these animals, picturing their potential suffering. "I have a really hard time dealing with people that have left animals in their houses," summed up one staff member. In many cases, they wanted to stretch these complaints into abandonment, despite overstepping the departmental definition of cruelty, so officers could rescue them. Dispatchers also knew that these cases were usually ignored by other agencies, neighbors, family, or friends, so they thought of themselves as the last line of defense if they could mobilize officers to intervene. One dispatcher described an abandonment case where a woman was committed indefinitely to a mental institution and left three cats behind without care. A sympathetic officer helped by going to her home every third day and leaving food, even though it was not a law enforcement situation: "These cases are the toughest, especially when somebody has no family or friends or anything like that because technically, it's not something we really deal with, we can't just go into the house, but we're not just going to say okay. We're not going to leave the cats in the house, so you try to find something to do."

Although these cases disturbed dispatchers who pictured starving animals in need of food, many officers were reluctant to help because they might have to illegally trespass to do so. One dispatcher bemoaned this dilemma in a case where the animal went unfed for three days: "I wanted some food under the door for the time being, just to do something to make sure it was okay, but I couldn't find anybody that would go there. The police were like, 'We can't go on the property.' But you know, it's tough because we hear that a lot: 'We can't go on to their property.' Well we can't either, but we're not going into their house you know." A few officers, however, could be relied upon to help in these situations. Trespassing on driveways or front walks could be seen as the smart thing to do, even though it was improper (Freilich et al. 1991). For animal-inclined officers, modest pressure from dispatchers often pushed them to behave smartly. And while improper, it was insignificant in comparison to more serious trespassing into yards or homes, making it seem more justifiable given their humane goals.

Abandoned animals were not the only emergencies handled by officers outside the formal definition of cruelty. There were "extreme" cases, in the eyes of dispatchers, that required the department to pick up veterinary bills, if the only other option was euthanizing the animal in question. Such a rare situation occurred when an officer was working on a dog-without-shelter case. The dog broke its leg, but the family could not afford the cost of fixing its injury. Officer Stan took the dog to the hospital and billed it to law enforcement because treatment was desperately needed. A dispatcher elaborated: "Those are tough ones too because you can't prosecute something like that. You can't say, 'Okay, if you can't afford to treat it, then you have to euthanize your dog.' Obviously, you're not going to say that to somebody. But obviously, it's not something you can do [pay for] all the time either."

Some situations were not emergencies, but dispatchers still wanted officers to check on the well-being of animals. For example, hearing about allegedly irresponsible owners could trigger stretching. One dispatcher talked about how she might stretch a call about an inadequate shelter into an investigable complaint when she had questions about the general competence of owners to care for animals: "He [respondent] might have a doghouse, but the person on the phone is still concerned that the house isn't adequate. You know, technically, if it has a

A complaint led officers to this dog, who was malnourished and inadequately sheltered.

doghouse and the dog looks healthy, then it's legal and there's nothing for us to look into. But if it just sounds like they are irresponsible owners and there is anything we can use that might be a violation—like they have a shelter, but it appears maybe it's inadequate—we would kind of sometimes stretch them into calls that we take." Another example of presumed irresponsibility would be owners who allowed their cats to have numerous litters of kittens. "Well, there's no breeding law. There is nothing that says that's cruelty to animals, but it could hurt the cat and it's irresponsible," added one dispatcher. Hearing about stray animals also prompted stretching. Helen, for instance, knew that the department could not pick up every stray cat, but was concerned about a report of one walking on a highway's median strip. She acknowledged that getting this cat fell outside the working definition of cruelty and was an animal control issue. Nevertheless, because of her own humane sensitivity, she asked an officer to look into the situation, fearing that other agencies would do nothing.

Knowing the department's reluctance to do work that smacked of animal control, dispatchers did not write up these calls as official complaints and instead informally sought help from sympathetic officers who worked near the endangered animals. Helen explained: "Officer Tim is probably not going to get the cat because there's no shelter in the area, but you tell Officer Betty there's a cat in the median and she's probably going to drive up and down the strip a few times just to pick up the cat. That's not in her job description. It's not really a law enforcement issue. It's basically a stray cat, but if she's in the area, she will probably stop by to pick it up." Putting the caller on hold, Helen called Officer Betty, who agreed to check on the cat. Had she declined, Helen would have called the local animal control office and implored them to help.

Mobilizing officers to intervene in these marginal cases became one of the dispatchers' informal job skills, requiring them to know which staff members would be willing to help animals and put aside legalistic definitions of cruelty. They also needed to make these requests sparingly and do so in a manner that did not put off officers. With these constraints dispatchers asked certain officers, more often the animal-inclined, to handle marginally acceptable complaints, and many obliged. As one dispatcher said of an abandoned cat complaint, "If it is an abandoned cat—the people moved away—the cat was left outside—technically our law enforcement officers are there to investigate abandonment. They are not an animal shelter. There are a couple that wouldn't pick up stray animals. 'If it's your cat, you go get it and bring it to the shelter.' But the majority of the officers will go and look for the cat and pick it up. There are even some who will go after work at night to go find the cat."

Of course, dispatchers did not stretch all calls. With more experience, they developed a sensitivity to spotting illegitimate complaints. Sometimes it was easy for them to spot callers whose concerns were unrelated to animal cruelty, but who tried to stretch them into complaints, nevertheless. A dispatcher commented: "There are definitely people who call us because they have some other hidden agenda, like they want us to harass their neighbor." Similarly, another dispatcher said of one caller: "He was trying to get it to be some sort of violation of cruelty—like the dog being in unsanitary conditions. But it turned out he was just really angry with his neighbor and was looking for any way to get the guy's dog taken away from him." Perhaps the most common situation in this regard was the caller who hoped to use law enforcement authority to manage interpersonal problems with family members. For example, a dispatcher described a caller who was having problems dealing with her son:

> I had a woman call me two weeks ago, her seventeen-year-old son had a rabbit and he wasn't cleaning the cage. I'm like, "You want us to have an officer go to your house and confront him for violating the law?" I'm like, "Why don't you try telling him to clean the cage and, if he refuses to, then tell him he's going to have to get rid of it and bring it to a shelter." And she was fine with that. She's like, "Oh, I could threaten to bring it to a shelter." I'm like, "You can tell him, if he's not going to care for it properly, you're going to take it and bring it to a shelter." I gave her the name of the shelter, where it was located so she had something to confront him with, and she was happy with that.

Problems between spouses also motivated people to stretch their calls and dispatchers might "catch" their lies: "Usually with complicated things—people calling on their ex-husbands—you can kind of catch onto that. Okay, there's a civil dispute going on over possession of the dog, so they are calling in a complaint on him trying to make him look bad so that they can get the dog. The more questions you ask, the more you realize things like that." Of course, despite their efforts to spot such lies, callers sometimes fooled dispatchers, as one noted: "Sometimes you never catch onto them. I think there's an animal completely in danger and the officer goes out there and it had a beautiful dog house, a beautiful yard, and I'll be like, 'Really?' You never know."

When dispatchers failed to stretch calls, it sometimes led to heated discussions with callers who insisted on seeing particular incidents as "cruel" and as meriting investigation. Having their complaints turned down left callers upset. "Some [calls] it's just 'no,' there's nothing I can do to make this sound like it's legitimate. They'll scream. They'll holler." A dispatcher elaborated: "People get angry sometimes with me and Lori [dispatcher] because we tell them that what they describe is not in violation of the law, so we can't do anything about it. 'Well what do you mean? So the dog's just going to sit there and suffer?' 'What do you mean he's suffering?' 'Well, he's cold.' 'Well, does he look okay? Does he look to be in good condition?' Sometimes you can't give them the results they want to see." Dispatchers felt that many callers had unrealistic expectations for what officers could do. As one dispatcher noted, "They [callers] live in a world that doesn't exist. Like I can make a phone call and everything will be wonderful. They seem to think that because we are the MSPCA, we have some universal power that's not regulated and we can sort of go above the law and take people's pets just based on our opinion that they should be removed."

To manage these situations, callers were told about the limits of humane law enforcement. Dispatchers felt "obligated" to explain what officers could not do so that callers had reasonable expectations of the department. One dispatcher discussed this problem and how she would handle a hypothetical call: "If someone's saying 'a dog is being left out in the rain and someone should come and just take this dog,' I'm not going to let them think that our officer is coming out there, and just the fact that the dog's in the rain, they're going to load it up in their truck. That's not going to happen."

Dispatchers also managed these situations by providing information or referrals. Callers, for instance, sometimes wanted to find lost animals or trap feral cats. Officers gave them traps, "but people don't want to do it and we can't do it." To assist callers and maintain a favorable public image for the humane society, they were referred to the local animal control office. One dispatcher explained this approach: "If you can't do anything to help that person, you want to give them some other outlet at least. You know, 'call animal control.' Because if you just say, 'I can't help you,' it doesn't look favorably on the organization as a whole. It may or may not, but at least you give them some other options that they haven't tried already." By making the referral, dispatchers clarified the common misunderstanding that humane law enforcement was animal control. As one said, "A lot of people think we're animal control, or they don't understand what we do—they consider us to be like a shelter. They don't realize that we have actual officers that are law enforcement officers. So sometimes you have to explain that, and then there's other people that know exactly who we are but they are not too sure how we handle things." If these educational approaches failed, dispatchers asked callers to talk with officers. One such caller contacted the law enforcement several times in a month, claiming that a neighbor's dog had no shelter. The dispatcher spoke directly to the investigating officer, who said that it was difficult to see the shelter in the back of the house but that it was acceptable. After hearing this explanation, the caller was still not satisfied and claimed that the shelter was inadequate. To placate the caller, the dispatcher then told her to call the officer on the case and talk to him.

In sum, dispatchers filtered calls through departmental and legal regulations, and decided on a course of action that depended on many factors, including their assessment of the caller's honesty, the availability of sympathetic officers, and their own humane sensibilities. Using all these criteria, dispatchers decided whether to contact an officer, with or without writing up a complaint, and to cast the case's fate into the officer's lap. For the most part the dispatcher's job was done at that point, while the officer's work just started. As a dispatcher noted, "When people call, I can't tell you what the outcome is or what's going to happen. I can tell you what may happen or what might not happen, but it all depends on what the officer sees when he goes there because what they are telling me over the phone isn't necessarily what the officer is going to see. Sometimes it's worse and not even comparable to what they were saying."

Compressing

Rookie officers, unsensitized to the practice of stretching complaints, assumed that reports of animal cruelty were true and subsequently took an adversarial stand toward respondents. As one officer recalled, "When I first started out, I remember you'd sit there and believe everything that people pass down to you. And you're always there, quick to jump on the respondent and never jump on the complainant."

As rookies gained experience they saw that many callers were not reporting animal cruelty, and the problems they described were more appropriately investigated by other agencies. Confronting these "bad" calls made officers suspicious if not cynical about the veracity of most complaints, whether the distortion or lying was intentional or unintentional, and whether it came from complainants themselves, animal control workers, dispatchers, or others. One officer explained: "When I was a rookie, I used to believe everything that people said. Then you get out there and you're shocked. 'My God, it does have a dog house!' And now I am like, 'This is what you're telling me, but I'll have to wait and see.' So I've become more cynical. I don't believe people even when they are telling me that they will be at the door at five o'clock." Another officer contrasted his attitude toward complaints with those of a rookie: "A lot of times, when you get the complaint, you turn around and in your mind you're saying that it's not possible that this complainant is telling the truth and her [rookie] attitude is that it's as bad as what the complainants are saying. You end up believing nobody. You don't believe the respondents and you don't believe the complainants."

The act of categorizing cases as "bad" was the opposite of stretching. While the latter practice inflated the working definition of animal cruelty, the former approach shrunk this definition by disqualifying reports as inappropriate for investigation. Complaint compression provided a counter-force to stretching. Out of this dynamic emerged the department's conception of a legitimate cruelty case.

Bullshit Complaints

Seasoned officers felt that many of their cases were not bona fide incidents of cruelty. These "bullshit" complaints, as they were called, had many sources. Some came from callers unconcerned about the well-being of animals. They had another "agenda," as one frustrated officer summarized, "There's all kinds of different reasons why people call you. To be honest with you, they don't always have the best interest of the animal at heart. They have their own agenda when they call." With this type of complaint, officers believed that callers lied and lodged unfounded cruelty reports for reasons having nothing to do with animal welfare or protection.

Some of these cases resulted from neighborhood feuds where complainants hoped that officers could remedy interpersonal problems that did not involve animal cruelty per se. Unable or unwilling to settle their own disagreements, they called in humane law enforcers to presumably manage problems that best might be considered matters of animal control. Barking dogs were often at the base of these complaints. In one case, the complainant alleged that a man was choking his dog. Although the respondent was not at home when the officer arrived, a neighbor, Nina, living in the above apartment came outside and spoke with the officer. Nina emphatically said that the respondent cared a lot for his two dogs and that he would never deliberately hurt them. She said that the dogs did bark a lot and agreed with the officer that the dogs were incorrectly tied to a rope that too easily became entangled. The officer also added that the dogs would benefit from having their water bowl secured to a post to prevent spilling. As the officer was leaving, the complainant—whose tattered dress, tattooed body, toothless grin, and unsteady gait gave her little credibility—came out of her house and told the officer that she saw the respondent choke his dog, but was told "to mind her fucking business" when she protested his actions. The officer headed toward his car, but quickly dispensed with her report after again meeting Nina, who said that Sally was "an alcoholic who had a fight with the owner's wife," suggesting that there was no basis to the choking complaint. The officer seemed convinced, based on his observations of the dog and conversations with Sally and Nina, that the respondent, at worst, played "toughly" with his dog. In his opinion, the complainant was really concerned about the dog's barking and could not resolve this problem due to her souring relationship with the respondent's wife.

Barking was not the only animal problem behind these frivolous complaints. For instance, landlords and tenants might have disputes over animals, with the former not wanting animals in their apartments or homes. Their hope was to use the cruelty complaint to get authorities involved in their struggle with uncooperative tenants. An officer described such a situation where the landlord expected officers to "clean house" by removing his tenant's animals: "If you get a landlord and the landlord is saying, 'I want the animals out of there. They're shitting and pissing all over the house.' If they're in good condition, and they're just shitting and pissing all over the house, then that's not an urgent situation from my standpoint. It might be from the landlord's standpoint, but it's not from my standpoint as it relates to the animal's wellbeing."

Other complainants sought to attack people or cause them trouble by getting law enforcement involved in falsified cruelty charges. As one officer explained, "These people, they don't care about the dog, but they get mad at the guy next door." "A lot of calls we get are fake. They are just people against each other and they just want to cause problems," said another officer who talked about how complainants in bullshit cases "don't always have the best interest of the animal at heart."

In one case, an officer investigated a complaint of "a dog that was a mess, disgusting looking," only to find a well-groomed dog that was old and overweight. After talking with the owner, the officer accepted his story that the complainant, who rented an apartment from the respondent, was upset because she was being evicted. As the investigating officer said, "There's nothing there. She [complainant] called to put the pins to her landlord because he was tossing her out." Using bullshit complaints as weapons was particularly evident when spouses wanted to "get even" and make life miserable for their former partners. Animals were used as pawns in these social struggles. An officer gave an example of a case where he felt no reason to be there. "It's a husband trying to get even with his ex-wife by getting the dog taken away. Yeah, the people are separating and the ex-wife's got the animals and the husband's saying that she doesn't take care of the animals and she says, 'Well, he's got a dog over at his girlfriend's place. You should take a look at that one. The dog hasn't been to the vet in two years.' So now you have to go and investigate him and it's just bullshit."

Rather than lying to officers about potential cruelty, some people had a genuine concern about the welfare of the animals but still reported baseless claims to the department. They did this for several reasons. According to officers, their concerns were "moral" rather than legal. "It's like everyone has their own definition of what proper care is, but all you can do is enforce the law. A lot of them are not really cruelty violations, but moral issues with animals . . . in other words, animals not being taken care of the way this person feels they should be taken care of. But it's not a violation of the law, either." Most moral concerns stemmed from complainants who cared more for animals than for people, claimed officers. As a police-oriented staff member said: "It bothers me when people say, 'Animals are more valuable.' We've gotten complaints where people will say that animals are a lot more valuable than a person's life." For example, one officer investigated a bullshit case where the caller did not like to see dogs in the rain. The complaint came in, "two dogs tied out in the pouring rain." It was a Friday afternoon, nearing the end of the workday, but the officer drove a long distance in torrential rain to check the animal. He knocked on the door and the partially dressed respondent answered, explaining that he worked nights and had been asleep. The officer identified himself and discussed the complaint. Surprised and angry, the respondent replied: "You son of a bitch" to which the officer said politely, "I understand what you're saying, but we have to respond." Reluctantly, the respondent got dressed, although without shoes, and went outside in the rain and mud to walk the officer around the back of the house only to see that both dogs had shelters. Reflecting on this case, the officer later said, "I was pissed because somebody was just pissed because the dogs were out. The dogs chose to stay out in the rain, but they both had their doghouses. They were both out in the rain looking at me."

Officers claimed that it was difficult to make these complainants "understand" that what they saw was not cruelty. One officer gave the example of a caller who claimed that a dog was a "bag of bones, in terrible condition and suffering, hardly able to walk and not being cared for properly." To the investigating officer, this "obviously wasn't a case of cruelty" because the animal was simply very old and normal for his advanced age, and the owner routinely took it to the veterinarian for care. "It's just an old dog. It's not suffering. It looks like hell. Its skin is terrible. It might be missing a lot of its fur or it might have a poor coat. It might be very thin, but there's not much they can do for the dog. It's just getting to be an old dog. From a cruelty standpoint of having to deal with the person that makes the complaint, a lot of times it's hard to make them understand, 'this is an old dog.'" Officers reminded complainants like these that respondents were within the law to let their animals live under the contested conditions, whether that involved a dog that preferred to lie outside rather than be in its shelter or another that was frail and thin because of old age.

Another reason for mistaken cruelty was that complainants based their reports on inadequate information. One officer used the example of a report about a dog being beaten. Although the law says that owners cannot cruelly beat their animals, the words "cruelly beat your animal" imply that owners can indeed hit their animals. What needed to be determined was whether hitting constituted a cruel beating, explained the officer. "When people call in situations where animals have been beaten, you have to differentiate between those individuals who hit their animals and those individuals that actually cruelly beat their animals. You have to be able to understand where that person who's making the complaint comes from, from a standpoint of are they just upset because a person hit their animal or did in fact the person actually beat their animal?" What might appear to be a beating might not be the result of any sort of malicious hitting, if complainants misperceive the behavior of animals and their owners. Such mistakes lead to false accusations of cruelty. An officer explained how this could happen, again using the report of a dog being beaten. The complainant may not have witnessed any "beating," but only heard a dog's wailing. "No, I didn't see them beat the dog, but the dog's screaming like it's being killed." The officer then goes to the respondent's home and gets a very different explanation of the "screaming." The latter says, "Oh, I didn't beat the dog. I just went over and grabbed it like this" and the dog starts "screaming and crying and carrying on and everything else." The officer continued: "They heard what they thought was the dog being beaten to death, but in fact the dog was just acting in—not an average way—but obviously in a way that would indicate to them that something is happening."

Mistaken cruelty could result from the complainant's lack of knowledge about animals. In one case, an officer explained why he thought someone was upset about puppies' not having water. He noted: "The woman complained because the dog had puppies and the puppies don't have any water to drink. Well, they don't drink water. They nurse when they are one and two weeks old. So the woman who is making the complaint obviously doesn't know." Officers thought that ignorance caused people to see suffering or cruelty when they did not exist. An officer gave the following example when driving past a horse farm: "A normal person would drive by and see that horse and see his back all sloped like that and think, 'Oh, my God, that poor thing.' But it's like a person. You've got horses that have sway backs. It's just from birth. Either they rode them too early or their spine isn't right, but they are fine. Most of the time when you see sway backs, they are old. Their spine just drops. And somebody will call a complaint in and say, 'Oh, the poor thing.'"

Complainants were not the only ones responsible for bullshit cases. So, too, were dispatchers, according to officers. They recognized that dispatchers were often the first people that callers talked to about their animal concerns, causing them to be at the peak of their frustration with particular situations. By the time officers investigated cases, some complainants were no longer so upset about whatever provoked them to call humane law enforcement. As one officer acknowledged, "They [dispatchers] are the first person that a respondent calls and they are upset. Quite often, people will call up and really give them a ration of bullshit, and when the officer talks to them, they're fine because they've gotten the frustration off their back. It just happens to be that they [dispatchers] are the first person they contact." Caught up in complainants' initial alarm and excitement, dispatchers were more likely to endorse rather than question their reports.

Officers also believed that dispatchers encouraged frivolous complaints because of the way they handled calls, making it easy for complainants to remain anonymous. Presumably, in their anonymity, callers were less hesitant to accuse others of cruelty than if they had to identify themselves. As one officer noted, "People do that [lie, distort] a lot of times. They will exaggerate things. They'll make up allegations that aren't true, especially if they're making anonymous complaints because it's easy for them to make all sorts of statements and there's no way of you getting back to them and saying, 'Why did you do that? Why did you say that if it weren't true?'"

Nor did dispatchers filter calls to eliminate many bullshit complaints, asserted officers. "They never want to say 'no' to anyone. Then don't tell them why this isn't something that we're going to look into. Instead, they'll just take any call and you do stuff that isn't necessarily law enforcement," claimed one officer. Similarly, another said: "No matter what, it's taken as a complaint, even if it has nothing to do with the MSPCA." Several officers argued that dispatchers were too willing to believe callers' reports. "It's very easy to sit there. You've never been out on the road, so every one of these complaints sounds serious to our dispatchers. And then when you get there, it's entirely different. The people are telling you this and you're dropping everything to go do that complaint, and you get out there, and there's really nothing to it. You just can't believe these people," said a frustrated officer.

Dispatchers took a more active hand in creating bullshit complaints, insisted officers. Well-intentioned but zealous at times, dispatchers prompted or coached complainants to report signs of mistreatment or cruelty to justify investigations in questionable or clearly inappropriate situations. The most common example of this was someone complaining about a barking dog. In such cases, officers believed that dispatchers would ask callers if the dogs were thin or had inadequate shelter. Many complainants, in turn, affirmatively replied to this "checklist" of problems to ensure that their complaints were followed up. One officer described this problem by comparing his own approach as a former dispatcher to those currently in the department. He claimed that when he worked as a dispatcher, "Someone will call up and say, 'This God-damned dog is barking.' When I was in the office, I'd say, 'We don't handle barking dog complaints. You have to call your animal control officer.' And you'd leave it at that. You'd just refer the people over." By contrast, he said dispatchers now say, "'Does the dog look good? Does the dog have water? Does the dog have food in front of him all the time?' And so the bells start ringing and they go, 'Oh well, they don't handle barking dog complaints, but if I say the dog looks thin or it doesn't have any water, or this and that, they can have someone go out there and check it out.'" Another officer described the problem of callers being "talked" into complaints: "The biggest complaint isn't that the dog's tied to a dog house. You find out that the biggest complaint is that it barks, and you find out they got talked into a complaint. Just barking—we can't go there unless there's something else wrong—the dog doesn't have any water or is thin or something. 'Oh yeah, the dog's thin.' Anything to get you there."

Officers did not place all the blame on dispatchers for talking up cruelty. A few believed "management" subtly pressured dispatchers to encourage and take as many complaints as possible. Somewhat cynically, a few officers theorized that this policy helped to document a heavy workload. As one officer said, "Part of the attitude is, 'We want to keep the numbers up. We want to get as many complaints as possible, so we don't want to turn people away.' Rather than tell people, 'Gee, we really can't take the complaint with the information you have right now,' they now say, 'you're going to have to call back when you get more information.'" Other officers argued that management did this because callers had been turned away by other agencies and animals needed assistance even if cruelty was not involved. Complainants may have unsuccessfully sought help with problems like barking from local animal control officers or police, only to "graduate" to the law enforcement department after exhausting these traditional avenues for help.

Most officers deplored baseless complaints, whatever their cause. Complainants could be difficult to work with and "demanding" because they were insistent and had unreasonable expectations, according to officers. One claimed that they would declare: "I want you to do this or I want you to do that" or "I don't care what you said, this is what it is." In response, the officer would say, in so many words, "Look, I go more by what I see than what I am told because of the fact that I know that so many times things get kind of twisted around a little bit and things are exaggerated." He would add, "I may not agree with the situation, but this is the way the law is." It was his opinion that "because a lot of people, unless someone is kissing their dog goodnight when they go to bed, they're not happy with the way an animal is being cared for. But it may not be a violation of the law." Although certainly not as extreme as "kissing a dog goodnight," another officer gave the example of a demanding complainant who was unhappy about a dog left outside at night without straw in its doghouse. The original complaint was for "no shelter," but after the officer found an adequate doghouse, the complainant insisted that the respondent should bring the dog into the house at night. The officer responded, "If he doesn't bring him in at night, now that he has the doghouse, there is nothing I can do." The complainant then pressured the officer to make sure that hay or straw was in the doghouse. The officer agreed to suggest this to the respondent, "but I can't make him put the hay or straw in."

Officers pointed out that complainants sometimes got angry with them because they did not take quick and decisive action when investigating cases. As one officer said, "Sometimes you're the guy who won't do anything. 'I called those people so many times and they just won't do a thing.' Even if you talk to the complainant, sometimes they still don't understand what you can do and what you can't do. They get the impression that you can just walk in and remove the animal if you feel like it." In one abandonment case, the complainant criticized Officer Ray for being "useless." "Some people think that we can just take animals, and that's it," said a frustrated Ray. He described what he had to do in one case to actually seize abandoned cats. The owner went away for about a week and casually left a small amount of food. To establish abandonment, he taped the respondent's door, to show that she had not reentered her home. Although he seized the cats, he returned them to the owner after she admitted to not leaving them without sufficient food. When he explained to the complainant that the cats had to be given back, "she hit the roof. She started swearing and she started crying and saying we were useless and 'I can't believe you are going to give the animals back.'" Ray replied, "I have no choice. What we can do is monitor the situation, make sure the cats are all right, and go from there." However, the complainant "didn't want any part of it. She was cursing me. This woman was furious. I said, 'I have no right to seize them.'"

Anger sometimes spilled over into name calling when complainants accused officers of being "inhumane" or "insensitive" because they did not do certain things for animals. As one officer noted, "With frivolous complaints, people will perceive that you don't have the proper level of sensitivity. You know, a complaint where there's nothing, except the person [complainant] thinks there's a serious problem. You don't particularly think that it is. In other words, you didn't find anything wrong there. That person may perceive that you don't have any humane sensitivity." As an example, another officer described the reaction she got when failing to revisit respondents' homes:

> If I didn't go back and do a recheck and the situation was still going on, the person who took the time to call us will just be like, "Well the MSPCA was out here and they didn't do anything. Why bother calling again if they are not going to do anything?" I get that a lot from people. I'll go out on a call and the person who made the complaint will call me back, and I'll tell them what I saw as a law enforcement officer. And they'll go, "Well, you just don't care. You didn't do anything about it." "As an officer there is nothing I can do. As a person I feel the same way you do." I hate having to tell people, "There really isn't a violation. There's nothing I can do." I can always try to educate them and talk to them, but if that doesn't work, then I have nothing else to go on.

This officer expressed her dismay at not being able to take more decisive action in such cases.

Not only could complainants be difficult to work with, but bullshit complaints were a "waste" of time that would be better spent investigating genuine cruelty allegations. The ideal norm in the department was for officers to assume that an animal's well-being was in jeopardy rather than the reverse. As one dispatcher noted, "Everything is pretty stretchable. The animal is given the most priority and the benefit of the doubt, so if there's even a possibility . . . As far as all the officers are concerned, they would rather go out and find nothing, than have me not take it." Real department norms revealed a different story. In practice many officers did not endorse this expectation, especially those having a police orientation. More commonly, they bemoaned bullshit complaints where their time and labor was misspent checking on animals not in jeopardy. One officer, for example, talked about a complaint of an "emaciated" dog: "I don't like it [bullshit case] because I get mad that I drive a long time to get there and there's . . . the complaint was an emaciated dog, open sores. And I go there and here's a beautiful German shepherd sitting on the couch with his owner watching *Oprah*, eating Burger King. That's just a waste of time. What if I choose to do a bullshit complaint and it was two hours away and I don't get back until late afternoon, and meanwhile, I could have been out on a case where cats are kept in a chicken-wire cage in the middle of a driveway in the blazing sun?" Another officer also spoke of "wasting time" on these cases:

> Say for instance, I get a call, "Dog out, no shelter." We drive down to the house and here's the dog, it's tied to a dog house. It's got plenty of shade and the dog's barking its head off, which happens quite frequently, especially where we take anonymous complaints. If I look and the allegations are totally unfounded, and I can see that, then there's no sense in me going up and approaching the people and saying, "Gee, I just want to let you know that I got a complaint that you didn't have shelter or shade for your dog." But I can see that's false, so why get the people all worked up over absolutely nothing at that point in time? You just drive off. And you've wasted your time being there and maybe taken you away from something else that may be more important. Especially if you've driven like an hour and a half to get someplace, and then you get another complaint, and you say, "Jesus, if I had

gotten here sooner it would have been better, and I wasted an hour and a half on this other thing that really had nothing to do with anything as far as that's concerned, other than maybe a barking dog complaint, which we don't have any jurisdiction over."

Despite the general resentment of bullshit cases, not everyone bemoaned them. Animal-inclined officers, in particular, were pleased to find well-treated animals, even if their investigations required extra time and effort. As one officer said, "Somebody calls up, 'Well, I'm not sure if it's skinny or not. I haven't seen him feeding it.' I'd rather have somebody go, even if it's me, and find out that the situation is okay."

Officers pointed out that exceptions justified the many worthless investigations; cases that appeared to be bullshit could turn out to be serious. "God forbid you got a call and you don't take it and an animal ends up dying or something. I don't care, send me out on all the bullshit complaints because you never know what's on the other end," noted one officer. Continuing, he said: "Seventy percent of people call up because they feel bad for the animal. The other 30 percent are calling because there's a dog barking and it's bugging them. And they only call in because the dog is making noise when they're trying to sleep. But what if the dog is barking because he's got no water or he's got no shelter? It's better to err on the side of the animal who can't call you himself and say, 'Get over here and help me.'" Such cases were often due to inarticulate complainants, explained one officer, who gave the following example: "Sometimes I'm completely fooled. I got this one call, 'It's barking. It's skinny.' And I got out there and the dog was like a rack

This emaciated dog was described by a complainant as "skinny."

of bones. And this woman just didn't know how to verbalize that over the phone. And I remember thinking, 'Wow, what if I didn't take that?'"

Also, bullshit complaints sometimes had serendipitous value because they led to the discovery of unexpected animal problems that did not necessarily involve cruelty per se. Respondents could be given advice that, if followed, resulted in furthering the well-being of animals. As one officer said, after investigating a case where he found no evidence to support the complaint: "That was a complaint that wasn't justified, but at least I went there and found another problem—the shelter—which could cause problems in the summertime if it's not corrected." In another complaint, an allegedly "thin dog" was found to be healthy and active, but the respondent revealed his plans to breed the dog and sell the puppies. This revelation gave the officer an opportunity to discourage unnecessary breeding by advising the respondent to take his dog to a local low-cost spay-neuter program. And in yet another case, the officer investigated a barking complaint only to find a dog that was "really thin. Who cares about the barking—the dog needed help."

Pain in the Neck Complaints

A second kind of bad complaint also plagued officers. They found "pain in the neck" calls difficult or frustrating to handle because of their ambiguity or because other agencies wrongly shirked their duties and "dumped" them on humane law enforcement. They were disqualified as cruelty but sometimes still attended to by officers.

Some ambiguity was administrative in nature. Dispatchers either could not get or failed to ask for certain basic information necessary for effective investigations, as happened when details of complaints were wrong or vague. For example, incorrect addresses for respondents or missing phone numbers for complainants meant that officers might not be able to find these people and manage these cases effectively. One officer, for instance, complained about not being able to follow up a complaint: "You know, what bothers me is to go into somebody's house and accuse them of kicking their dog when it's an anonymous call. I feel like a jerk because they get mad. 'What do you mean, I kicked my dog?' 'Well, somebody called.' 'Who called?' 'Well, they didn't leave a name.' You have a tough situation." Muddled descriptions of cruelty made it difficult for officers to assess their seriousness. Officers frequently investigated cases that had few details about the alleged cruelty, making it difficult to assess whether abuse occurred. In one complaint, for instance, "someone saw a dog in the car. They didn't know whether it was distressed. Didn't notice whether it was panting. The only thing they noticed was that there was a dog in the car. They didn't even notice how long it was in there and called in." Sometimes the complaint was simply wrong, as one officer illustrated: "You get out on an unsanitary condition call and it's an odor problem that has nothing to do with unsanitary conditions. The odors just permeate an establishment or a yard or something like that, and yet the place is perfectly clean."

Other ambiguity involved cases that required an officer's subjective decision-making skills. Rookies quickly discovered that even apparently identical complaints could not always be handled the same way. Two similar complaints involving the same allegations might call for very different management. Officers bemoaned that there were few "cut and dry" cases to investigate. "That's what makes the job difficult. There's no real cut and dry situations. Like when a landlord wants an animal removed, I pretty much tell them, 'I'll determine if there is a violation of the law, and then I'll tell you where we're going to proceed from there.' In some cases, I'll tell the landlord it's their responsibility to remove the animals. In some cases, I will take the animals." Sometimes factors unrelated to respondents resulted in the same kind of complaint being managed in different ways. For example, it was not always clear to officers when they should enforce the law if there were "unsanitary conditions" for animals. The law forced officers to decide not only what constituted sufficient harm due to inadequate sanitation, but when unsanitary conditions were normal or at least reasonable. Many times they ignored these conditions, depending on the season. In the spring, for example, officers tolerated what otherwise might be a complaint to enforce. "When the frost is coming out of the ground and there's mud and shit and crap and everything else, what are you going to tell the people they're going to have to move their horses inside the house?" Similarly, unsanitary conditions might be tolerated in the winter. "If you're getting freezing rain and snow and sleet and the dog shits and before the people can clean it up, it's impacted in ice . . . in some cases, it's not unsanitary. It may look like hell, but it's not unsanitary because it's all covered in ice and snow."

Officers believed that they had many more complaints that were not "black and white" compared to regular police, even though studies of the latter suggest otherwise (Bittner 1990). As one officer explained, "We deal with a lot of gray areas, whereas with most police violations, it's fairly black and white. It's either a problem or it's not a problem. And if it's a problem, many times you have a lot you can do because you witnessed it yourself or you have firsthand knowledge, and you don't have to rely on all these other people to get involved to get your job done." Another officer agreed: "I think most of the stuff that police departments deal with is black and white. It's either a violation or it isn't, which is what's so difficult about this job. Everybody has an opinion as to what proper care is, as to what proper shelter is, and it's just a very gray area. It boils down basically to someone's opinion if it's a violation or not." One officer gave "beating" as an example of the ambiguity of their cases, noting: "The problem with a dog beating is when does it become a beating and when is it just discipline? It's very difficult when you go out on a case where people claim they were beating the dog because they are disciplining it. Where is that line where they cross over and actually beating it?"

Whether or not they were forced to use more discretion and judgment than regular police, humane officers interpreted the meaning of the anti-cruelty code on a case by case basis. Their perception that cruelty work had even greater ambiguity than regular policing had some truth, since the body of law for human crime was so large and detailed compared to the paltry laws about cruelty. Although animal police grumbled about how frustrating it was to interpret and apply the law, the very ambiguity that stymied them also provided an opportunity to clarify and extend the meaning of cruelty or at least humane treatment. Many times, they alone made this decision, since experts could not always clarify the ambiguity of the law or its "gray areas." One officer gave the example of proper shelter for horses: "Take horses outdoors. What is proper shelter for a horse? If you talk to a veterinarian, some of them will say that trees, thick cover like that is okay—that's proper shelter. Other vets will say you need three sides and a roof. Some vets like them locked in a barn, some vets don't."

In lieu of such help, officers fell back on informal understandings about what their peers did. One officer, for example, explained that the law says "you should feed and water your animal," but it does not say that dogs should be constantly provided with water. However it was a departmental norm for officers to "recommend" that owners provide dogs with water twenty-four hours a day. "Nowhere in the law does it say you have to do that. It says you have to feed and water the animal enough to maintain it in good condition and you have to give it enough water so that the dog doesn't get dehydrated. But we recommend more . . ." When there was not a consensus in the department about what the law meant, officers individually made this interpretation. One gave the example of a dog getting "adequate shelter." In its ambiguity, officers defined what they thought constituted sufficient protection for animals or by contrast, what was neglectful or even cruel. "I might not be concerned about the size of the opening of a doghouse, but that becomes a judgment call on my part. Another officer might say, 'No, I want a bigger hole.'" The same officer spoke about how he urged owners to add straw to doghouses to keep animals warm and to make sure that they were kept dry.

Some officers blamed dispatchers for pain in the neck complaints because they made it easy for callers to be anonymous and rarely pushed them for details. One officer lamented the way things used to work in the department when such calls were quickly dismissed:

> When I worked in the office, I would just matter-of-factly take the complaint and I'd ask for their name. Then, if they hesitated or showed some reluctance, I'd explain to them, "We don't give out the names of people who call us." Then, if they really push that, I'd say, "Well, you can remain anonymous if you choose to remain anonymous, but by remaining anonymous, this is what happens . . . and if we can't find it, then so forth and so on." A lot of people would give you their name. The way they deal with them now in the office is they say to them, rather than saying, "What is your name?" they say to them, "Would you like to leave your name or would you like to remain anonymous?" If you were approached that way, you'd say, "Well, Jesus, I don't have to leave my name." What would you pick? The other thing is they take phone numbers, but they don't take addresses, which is a problem because sometimes you can tell a lot by having a person's address. But I know for a fact that they're not asked for their addresses.

Another officer wanted dispatchers to use a checklist so they could elicit certain information from complainants, including their name, address, and phone number. He described his "gripe" with them:

> Not, "Would you like to leave your name and number?" Because if someone asked me that, "No, why should I?" But if you say, "Name and number?" and it's confidential, I've never had anyone turn me down when I've said that. I may have to explain why I need it. Then

take the complaint and ask them all these questions: "Have you called animal control before?" And try to ferret out some of the stuff that is obvious bullshit. We get a lot of vague complaints. They take crummy complaints. That's frustrating for us, especially if it's anonymous because you don't have anyone to call back. You just go, "I can't do anything else. I don't have anyone to call. You didn't give me enough information." "Well, I didn't even think of that." It's like, "Well, think of that."

Pain in the neck complaints had other causes. Some should have been taken care of by organizations that inappropriately delegated or referred them to humane law enforcement. These cast-off complaints irritated officers, not because they made for extra work per se, but because they challenged their identity as professional law enforcers. Once again, they were treated like animal control workers, and they abhorred this association.

For one, humane officers got pulled into animal-related sanitation problems not managed by local authorities. "They are just a way to shuttle off a problem to another agency and keep it out of town," noted one officer who gave the following example of a town shirking its duty: "We get a lot of odor problems—sanitation problems with big farms. It's something that the town should be doing. It's a sanitation problem. You go there, the animals might be okay. You talk to them about some of the sanitation, but it really isn't a cruelty thing. It's more a town's responsibility. It gets pushed off on us. 'We call the MSPCA.'" Another officer complained about having to pick up and transport the decomposed body of a beagle, a dirty job that in his opinion should have been done by the local animal control officer: "It really bothered me. I just don't like seeing something like that so decomposed. I couldn't look at it. I put it in the bag and I had to carry it about a quarter of a mile. I had it double bagged, but it was dripping on me. I couldn't have just left it there. I wouldn't have felt right. Plus the woman was standing behind me saying, 'I can't believe that the animal control officer wouldn't take this.' He left it there. I didn't want to do it either, but . . ."

Local authorities also dumped nuisance complaints on animal police. As one officer pointed out, "A lot of them [complainants], it's that they are getting no satisfaction from their animal control officer. So they'll call us. 'The dog barks all the time,' and we'll say, 'Sorry, there's nothing we can do about that. We do cruelty.'" Or as another officer said: "A lot of times people will call with an ulterior motive—they have already called animal control and they have done nothing. We get a good percentage of that, and that's frustrating because it's not our job and you get out there and we are driving a long way to come up there when it's probably going to be a waste of time." Like bullshit complaints, these cases often stemmed from long-standing tensions among neighbors over animal-related problems where complainants hoped that humane officers, as a last resort, could use their authority to remedy such situations. As one noted, "Complainants just think that we're going to go out and just seize the animals, maybe just listen to them, and seize them and that solves their problems."

For instance, one officer investigated a case where the complaint of inadequate shelter actually masked several years of tension between neighbors over a barking dog. He examined the dog and spoke with the respondent and concluded that the dog did not need a backyard shelter because the weather was good and the owner claimed to take the dog into his house. As the officer was driving away, the complainant approached the vehicle and, with great exasperation, spoke for fifteen minutes about her failure to get the respondent to silence his dog and her inability to receive help from local authorities. At first, the complainant claimed that "when it's ninety-five degrees, that dog's just where he is. That's a twenty-foot chain, there's no shade, there's no water . . ." She spoke about her efforts to correct the sun and water problems and explained to the officer what she said to the respondent: "'He [the dog] has no water.' This is what he said to me. 'He knocks it over.' I said, 'Get a five-gallon bucket and put that out there. He won't knock that over. At least he's got some water. Move your chain. You've got trees over here for shade. Move your chain.' 'Well, I don't want to ruin the rest of the grass.' 'You know, officer, you are going to have to help out here and do something because the situation is not going to change.'" The officer then pointed out to her that the dog had water and that he was brought in at night, according to the respondent. The woman, appearing very frustrated, spoke about how it bothered her to see the dog ignored by its owners:

> I love dogs. I love animals. I've had them all my life. You can walk right over to him [the dog]. He wants attention. They're an elderly couple. They got him. He has a bad heart. He tried walking him and the dog knocked him right down. So the dog's never been walked. Never. He's always on the chain. I feel bad for the dog, personally. The dog is out there for hours. He barks his head off, and no one is

around, and that's why he's barking. They [dogs] need a lot of attention and unfortunately they [respondents] are getting on in years and they just don't have the time, you know. The other night he [respondent] was out there under a tree in a chair and the dog—bark, bark, bark—and I went around the corner and I said: "You can't hear that Bob?" And he got up, moved his chair, sat right alongside of the dog, and the dog stopped [barking]. All he [dog] wanted was for him to pet him. How do you make him [respondent]? He's not a bad dog. I love the dog. It's just unfortunately I think he's [respondent] too old to have it. I think he's told me he's tried to give him away a couple of times, and I don't know if the dog keeps coming back or if nobody wants him because he does bark a lot. We've approached him in a nice manner and said, "Frank, you're getting on." "Well," he says, "It's for protection." My sentiment is, if you want protection, get a security alarm 'cause that's not what pets are for. He's a good neighbor. I've been here for years, but you know, we've approached him and said, "Look, maybe you're getting too old because the dog needs a lot of attention. You can't give it the attention or the time, you know."

Clearly, the essence of her complaint reflected long-standing disapproval of the respondent as an adequate pet owner in the complainant's eyes because he allegedly paid little attention to his dog.

As the officer patiently listened to her, the complainant finally focused more on how the "dog will bark continuously." She claimed to have tolerated the barking for a number of years until it reached a point where she and others in the neighborhood could no longer live with it. Elaborating, she noted, "You know, I didn't want to do it at this point, but the other day we were out there and it got to a point where the dog barked three hours straight. I timed it. For five years, we've been putting up with this. My pool abuts his backyard. I have a pool and I can't lay out there. I have a deck that goes right in the back. I can't sit on the deck at night to have supper. I can't go out and read my paper. I can't have breakfast out there."

The complainant claimed that she delayed calling humane officers because in addition to being neighborly (i.e., having the courtesy not to complain formally and to work out the problem with the respondent), she exhausted the help of local authorities who did nothing to improve this situation. She went on to say that the local animal control officer told her that he was unable to do anything as long as the dog barked only during daylight hours. The humane officer then described how the law defines a "nuisance" animal and how she could make a written complaint to her board of selectmen, local chief of police, or county commissioners. Although the barking was a nuisance for the respondent and her neighbors, it served more as a trigger for this woman to make a complaint to humane law enforcement after trying unsuccessfully to mobilize help elsewhere.

As these examples demonstrated, officers usually dealt with frivolous or baseless complaints rather than ignore them. They approached these cases as professionals, conducting investigations when appropriate and helping animals when possible. Their response was akin to that of regular police, who find that much of patrol work does not involve law enforcement. Order maintenance and service delivery, unrelated to legal mandate, demand the majority of their time (Meehan 1992). So, too, with humane officers. Hence, they sometimes did work that should have been handled by other organizations or groups in the state, in particular, animal control. And, like bullshit cases, sometimes investigating pain-in-the-neck complaints led to the discovery of harmful situations for animals that could be rectified or improved. Additional problems unmentioned in the original ambiguous complaint might be found. In a complaint reporting a "dog tied up outside," an officer found other problems with the animal. He recalled: "Not really cruelty, but it was definitely neglect. Very badly matted, tied out to a dog-house."

Although officers approached these cases as professionals, most them. Maligning these complaints, however, misses the big picture or social context that produces these calls. All officers, whether police-oriented or animal-inclined, focus on what is in front of them to make sense of these annoying and sometimes perplexing complaints. They blame complainants for being ignorant or caring too much for animals, they blame dispatchers for not collecting more information or for not screening out calls, they blame management for encour-

Investigating a "dog tied up" led to the discovery of a badly neglected animal.

aging this indulgence, and they blame other organizations for not doing their jobs. Throughout all this blame, they see cruelty's meaning trivialized—it is twisted into being a weapon, it is misapplied to very ambiguous situations, or it is stretched to meet inflated humane expectations. However, bemoaning these complaints as senseless shortchanges their social significance. They are not just caused by individuals misconstruing a dog's wail as evidence for abuse; they are also caused by a social breakdown in the relationships between neighbors or within families, a breakdown that often reflects problems that are long-standing and difficult to resolve. According to Perin (1988), problems with pets tell us much about humankind. When the bond is questioned between people and animals, much is revealed about our collective life. Dog problems, in particular, seem to come between people and bring out the worst in them. Commonly, these problems are long-standing and difficult to resolve, "ungluing the neighborhood." Animals are not the real problem. People are really complaining about people. Quarreling over barking dogs, fretting over thin dogs standing in the rain, or stewing over cats roaming through gardens are all signs of a loss of social trust in America. While officers and dispatchers search for animal cruelty in the complaints they get, and find it unremarkable or wanting in most cases, they miss what is remarkable and apparent in these calls; namely, that social relationships are failing or in serious trouble. Neighbors have changed to enemies, spouses have turned into adversaries, and parents have become alienated from their children. In the pain in the neck or bullshit complaint, officers may not be finding much cruelty, but they are seeing profound social breakdown.

In the course of handling thousands of complaints each year, dispatchers and officers decide what gets counted as animal cruelty. Dispatchers "err" on the animal's side by stretching most calls that come into the department so they can be officially regarded as cruelty complaints or at least investigated by officers. Although dispatchers are well aware of the technical definition of cruelty, by taking the caller's perspective, they give expression to a notion of cruelty that goes beyond its strict legal definition. In the end, such stretching by dispatchers creates a very broad working definition of potential cruelty and ensures that animals in need are not ignored. This creates a wide humane safety net.

However, as officers manage complaints, they find that such stretching swamps them with cases that have nothing to do with animal abuse or that do not meet the technical definition of cruelty. Because they feel constrained by the application of law, officers often find this broad definition of cruelty to be unacceptable. Viewing some complaints as bullshit or a pain in the neck, and others not, was their way of differentiating valid complaints from others. Professionals from other fields do this too when they classify some of their cases as problematic (e.g., Mennerick 1974; Sanders 1994). For example, physicians consider bad patients to be those who are undesirable to work with because they have unreasonable expectations for help, complicated medical conditions unresponsive to treatment, or character flaws or moral inadequacies (Lorber 1981). Just as physicians disqualify problematic patients from legitimately occupying the patient's role, humane officers disqualify respondents named in bad complaints from legitimately occupying the role of animal abuser. By classifying some complaints as bad, officers can compress the abundant pool of potential cruelty created by dispatchers and complainants, in turn clarifying the meaning of cruelty and reaffirming officers' law enforcement identity. Ultimately, the working definition of animal cruelty—as opposed to some legal or abstract moral definition—is what officers consider appropriate to investigate, the bulk of which are "no food, water, shelter" cases.

As the bedrock of cruelty work, such cases pose a serious challenge to the identity of animal police. They are a far cry from the kinds of egregious cruelty officers expect to investigate when they join the department. And particularly for police-oriented officers, cases involving inadequate food, water, and/or shelter are reminders that their law enforcer status is precarious, since the work they do on simple neglect complaints is often very close to that of animal control. This explains why many officers deplore extreme and heinous cases at the same time that they also welcome them. These cases remind officers why they entered this field and validate their idea of what humane law enforcement should be. One such case involved a respondent who killed a dog in cold blood. The investigating officer compared it to his regular cases: "These are more important because they are violent. They give me a sense that I am doing law enforcement work. When I come out to a no-shelter complaint, I'm more like a regular dog officer." The trick is for officers to see abuse in these ambiguous or questionable cruelty complaints, and then see themselves as law enforcers in the process.

3

Sizing Up Situations

> The danger comes from these daily dry routine jobs where that 99th one—you know it's somebody in their house, someone complains about a dog without food, water, shelter, and you walk into a crack house or you come up and the guy has a mental problem and a gun and you don't know about it. And he sees your uniform and that's it. It's all over. That's where your danger is.

Whether officers viewed complaints as good or bad, they investigated most to rule out mistreatment of animals. They did this because some callers failed to do justice to cruelty and under-reported the nature and extent of harm done to animals. In medical terms, this would be analogous to the "false negative," where pathological findings are discovered despite test results indicating no problem. To ensure that these false-negative reports were not ignored and to handle those complaints that accurately reported cruelty, officers tried to observe animals and talk face-to-face with respondents.

However, it was rarely a simple black-and-white matter to determine whether cruelty occurred. Constructing a picture of the respondent-animal relationship called for officers to make judgment calls and inferences about what happened. Harm was not always apparent during investigations; tell-tale signs of abuse might not exist because assaults on victims took place hours or days before or respondents might lie to officers and evade their questions, for example. Far from being a simple inspection of an animal's status, human problems made investigations even more trying. Officers sometimes found themselves in complicated and tense interpersonal situations that made them deal with a host of problems having more to do with the breakdown of social interaction than with animal cruelty per se. Despite these problems, officers pieced together what information they could cull and infer from their visits to tell the animal's story.

Telling Their Stories

Officers represented animals and "read" their status to determine whether they had been treated cruelly according to law. To a certain extent, reading their status simply called for direct inspection of animals, and sometimes this was relatively easy to do even without special veterinary knowledge or experience. As one officer noted, "It's like any animal. If you go and see a cow that's laying down, but he was bright and everything, that's okay. But you might go and find a cow that's laying down and he's just kind of listless and just looking at you like 'I don't feel good.' They just kind of tell you. Same with their feet. If they are not feeling good, they're going from foot to foot. They kind of balance the weight on the soreness." Another officer claimed that while he was not a horse "expert," there were "extreme" cases where cruelty was obvious, despite what respondents said to the contrary. The latter can "get very technical about this type of medical condition and I don't know what the hell they're talking about," said this officer, "but I know enough to feel that there is cruelty when it is extreme. You don't have to be an expert to look and see a starving horse and know that it's starving. Whether it's not being fed properly or it's a starving horse because it's not getting proper medical attention, really doesn't come into play. It's still a starving horse." Easily read cases were rare. Reading an animal's status to detect abuse was usually a complicated task.

Reading Problems

For one, officers were constantly reminded that animals could not articulate their mistreatment. By contrast, human abuse victims could report their abusers, although they might be reluctant to do so, fearing retaliation. The voicelessness of animals was very apparent in one case of an alleged dog beating; the woman present had been beaten by her boyfriend, the respondent. The officer investigating this case compared the dog to the girlfriend: "I feel badly for the girl and just as badly for the dog. But at least she can speak up and she's got a family that wants to help her."

The fact that abuse could be hard to see created a problem. Cases of injured animals—those with broken legs for example—were easier for officers to investigate and pursue cruelty charges. More commonly, evidence of harm was not present. Among others, animals "tossed" or "kicked" did not always show physical signs of cruelty by the time officers examined them. By contrast, human victims more likely did. As one officer said, "With animals often it's difficult. Say I get a complaint that someone beat their animal, and you get out there and there's no signs that the animal is injured. It's very hard to determine bruising on that animal unless there is an autopsy. Where, say I get a complaint as a police officer that someone's abusing their kid, and you get out there and he's got bruises all over him, then you know that the bruises are consistent with what you've been told."

The reverse also could occur. What looked like abuse might not be. For one, animals could act as though they were recently abused when they were not. To illustrate, an officer talked about how a "timid" dog's behavior can mistakenly point to cruelty: "Sometimes an animal will indicate that it's abused by the manner in which it acts, but you can't always go by that. There's timid dogs that I know of. You may go out to a house and speak to someone about abusing their dog and approach the dog and have the dog cower and put its tail between its legs and crunch down and everything else, and say, 'Gee, it looks like this dog is being abused.' And it might be abused in some cases, but in other cases it might just be the animal's disposition."

Problems assessing cruelty meant that officers needed special skills and information to make sense of complaints. Having veterinary or first-hand knowledge of certain species made it easier to read some animals. Those officers having this background were less reliant on respondents' reports and more confident about their own assessments. For example, one officer felt that he had more experience than did his peers with horses and, because of this, believed respondents could not fool him when dealing with these cases. As he noted, "I think it comes with experience over the years. I was raised around horses, so I know horses. I can go into a stable and somebody will say, 'blah, blah, blah.' And I'll say, 'Look, before you make a fool of yourself, don't even tell me that. I've been around too long.' And it's a good feeling, you feel sure of yourself. A lot of the guys at work have no knowledge of horses, but they may have it with dairy, or they may have it with dogs." Some animals, like birds or reptiles, were "tough" to assess. This problem was compounded when officers investigated cases of exotic animals. For example, a report of ostrich abuse was made to the department. The investigating officer talked about how he had to use the Internet to get information about ostriches: "I looked some stuff up on the internet when I first started dealing with this guy, just so I could have kind of a basic knowledge about what was going on." Even with domestic animals, like dogs, officers sometimes required special knowledge to assess cruelty. In one complaint, a respondent was accused of having a "thin" dog. When the officer arrived at the respondent's home, he observed the dog from the driveway and said: "That dog's a little bit on the lean side, but it's an active dog. That's another thing that makes the job difficult in that you pretty much have to know all sorts of different animals [breeds] and you have to be able to recognize that this is an active dog, so it probably wears off its food, and is fairly muscular and the whole works." At other times, the proper assessment of cruelty required knowledge of the behavior of specific animals. During one investigation, a dog appeared to be in some distress, as it limped and cried. The investigating officer said of the dog's behavior: "That particular puppy is the type of puppy that when it sees people, it starts whining and crying. I'm familiar with that puppy from other times I've been there. Whether the puppy is suffering or in pain or not, I don't know. But it's certainly something that, if it hasn't been to the vet, it should be taken to the vet as soon as possible."

Even with such veterinary knowledge, officers might turn to complainants for more information, "otherwise, it's just one word against the other." However, with anonymous complaints, officers could not ask more questions. A staff member gave the following example. He said that a caller might say, "I saw my neighbor beating the dog. He's out there beating him with a stick." If the caller remains anonymous, fearing the neighbor, and the dog appears to be well and unabused, the officer assumes the respondent will deny doing it. "There is nothing that we can really do. The dog can stay there and get beat every day and there's nothing we can do about it. We can't, even if we legitimately believe her that this is happening. If the dog isn't showing any signs, you have no one willing to come forward and write a statement as to what they've seen, and the guy denies it, you have nothing to go on."

Officers also turned to respondents to learn more, although this too could be difficult and frustrating. One problem was their isolation when tracking down respondents. They usually investigated cases by themselves and spent long hours driving alone to respondents' homes or businesses. This meant that they had no one to talk to in the field when troubled by their work. As one said, "You leave the respondent's home, and if you have a forty-five minute ride to your next call, you're thinking. It's a very emotional job because you are alone a lot. You spend way too much time with yourself." Another officer, who could visit the law enforcement department during the day, felt that, unlike most of her colleagues, she could "turn around and say, 'Oh Helen, you wouldn't believe what a jerk this woman was.' You can blow off steam that way. The people on the road can't do that." Just finding and talking to respondents could take a lot of time and effort. Long drives also frustrated officers because they not only entailed overtime work, but frequently turned out to be wild goose chases. "They send you out to Timbuktu," bemoaned one officer. One of her colleagues got a call at three o'clock in the afternoon to investigate an abandoned animal case that took two hours by car to reach. "A woman was supposedly in a loony bin and they just found that her animals were inside the apartment all that time. I finally found the woman—she came back the night before and was taking care of the animals. I said, 'Why didn't somebody know this, it was a long wasted trip.' I mean, she came back the night before!" Sometimes respondents were not home when officers investigated cases, requiring return visits to speak with them and to observe their animals. "You go back and forth, like a yo-yo, sometimes three or four times on the same complaint," commented one officer. Similarly, another officer complained about "going around in circles" with many of his cases. It was equally aggravating to speak with low-level employees or children, when owners, managers, or adults were unavailable. In one case, an officer made repeated visits to a farm to check on the health of cows, whose hooves had overgrown, only to find farm hands who claimed to have relayed earlier messages from the officer to the manager of the farm. As the officer recounted, "I'll go there and speak to the foreman. He'll say, 'I'll get a hold of Mr. Smith [manager] and let him know you were here.' Then I talk to Mr. Smith and he'll say, 'Oh no, I never got the message, but I'll check it.' Then I'll go back to the foreman and he'll cover, 'Well, I left the message.' Until you know that each one got the message, you just have to play games."

Respondents could be home but disregard officers by not answering the door or not returning their requests to be called, as indicated on business cards left in mailboxes. This happened repeatedly to one officer with the same respondent: "I've got this woman in Lake City. She is seventy years old and she's like an old hermit. Like the police said, you have to catch her there. She's not going to answer you. Sometimes she's inside, so you have to bang on the door, keep bang-ing until she gets sick of hearing it and she might come to the door." In another case, the officer made six visits, leaving cards each time, only to have the respondent not call back. On the seventh visit, again no one answered, despite clues that someone was home, such as a car in the driveway, open windows, and television sounds. He telephoned the respondent from his car three times while parked outside the latter's home, only to get an answering machine. Of course, when finally confronting repondents, it could be very unpleasant to meet them. As one officer said, "You leave your house and do complaints all day and go home, and the only people you see all day are the people who don't want to see you. They may yell at you, curse you, or slam the door on you."

Unpleasantness aside, reading respondents could be as complicated and disappointing as reading animals. In most cases, officers ultimately reached respondents by telephone or in person. When they did, cruelty was rarely simple to determine. Rather, they read respondents to construct a "story" of abuse and a "picture" of the abuser. By definition, respondents were not a voice for the animals in question. In fact, to clarify their role in cruelty investigations, officers sometimes explicitly made this point to respondents. In one case, the complaint alleged that the respondent kicked his dog. When the officer spoke with the respondent, he became angry about the allegation, claiming never to have mistreated his dog and asserting that the neighbor lodged the complaint because "she didn't like black men with Pit Bulls." To avoid taking sides with the complainant or respondent, the officer affirmed that he only represented the animal.

Although officers tried to be impartial when they did this, rookies soon learned that respondents commonly distorted the truth, at least to some degree, or blatantly lied. As one officer put it, "You show up in uniform, and people are not going to say, 'Okay, I did it. Take me to jail or prosecute me,' or something like that. It is not at all unusual for them to put their own little spin on things." Similarly, another officer said: "They deny it. It is very rare to have somebody admit to killing their animal." Compounding the lying, respondents always had justifications or excuses for their supposed abuse, much like the accounts of social deviants who try to explain away their questionable behavior (Scott and Lyman 1968). As one frustrated officer noted, "Respondents will tell you the most bizarre excuse for what they did. You just go, 'If [only] you could put that energy into something productive, instead of making up the cockamamie story of why you couldn't care for this animal. You're actually a bright person. You are channeling it the wrong way.'" One common justification, for example, was for respondents to blame their actions on the animals, thereby denying responsibility but acknowledging wrongdoing. According to one officer, "People always tend to blame their animals for something violent like that. 'The dog tried to bite me,' or 'the dog tried to do this or tried to do that,' or 'the dog tried to run away.'" Although less common, respondents also tried to excuse their actions by accepting responsibility while denying wrongdoing. One excuse, for instance, was for respondents to say that they were "only" disciplining or training their animals rather than harming them.

Getting Gut Feelings

Like regular police (Brooks 1993), humane officers evaluated the moral character of suspects. These evaluations gave officers a "gut" impression of respondents, including their trustworthiness and concern for animals, despite the lies, justifications, and excuses. According to one officer, "You get to know who you can trust and who you can't trust, or if what somebody's telling you is true or not, if it's in the ballpark even." Newcomers learned to trust this "gut" feeling, even after they got "burned." As one recalled, "You don't trust anyone, you don't believe what anyone tells you and they still burn you. And you go, 'This is why I don't trust anyone. I should have known.' I did about two months ago and it worked out okay. Sometimes you go, 'Oh, my God, I can't even trust my gut anymore.' But usually it's pretty good." This gut feeling was important because it influenced how officers approached and handled cases, telling them, for instance, whether it will be easy or hard to work with respondents. An officer explained, "You can get a pretty good feel for people when you are there. Every now and then you find one that can really bullshit you. But you look at the house and you look at what's going on in the property and the care of the animal, and what the problem is, and that pretty much can reflect whether you can work with them or whether or not you're going to have a problem there."

Officers gathered information to generate these gut feelings, or as one said, "You try and see everything," noted one officer. This judgment took shape from the moment officers got complaints and started learning about respondents, even if what they learned was sketchy and secondhand. For example, respondents' names and addresses, as well as the nature of complaints, revealed ethnic group membership. According to the department's oral culture, members of certain groups were difficult to talk to and likely to mistreat their animals. This expectation made officers extra wary of reports from them. In this vein, one officer talked about her expectations of Portuguese respondents: "Portuguese are the worst. It's not that they are cruel. It's just that their dog is a dog and it lives outside. It gets fed bread and scraps. They're the worst for the way they keep their animals." Similarly, in a case of "inadequate shelter," another officer said, "It's kind of a common way for them [Portuguese] to keep the dog, but not acceptable as far as our standards. The dog is in the doghouse all the time, but it stinks. I tend to have that with the towns that I deal with."

If not their ethnicity, respondents' occupations tipped off officers to their likely behavior. Staff members pointed to pet store owners and "horse people" as especially likely to lie: "They'll tell you anything, just to get rid of you, especially if they know you don't know a damn thing. If you go to, like, horse people, if you go into a stable, and you see something. Horse people know horse people, and by certain questions you ask, they know already, 'this guy doesn't know what he's talking about.' 'Oh, yeah, that's nothing. Don't worry about it . . . da, da, da.'"

Seeing how respondents lived also shaped their expectations. Officers believed it was easy to spot the homes of respondents because they usually were the most poorly kept in the neighborhood. As one officer said, "There may be five beautiful houses, and there's just that one house that needs work, and you know you're headed there." A colleague elaborated, saying that the dilapidated condition of many respondents' homes was not the result of low income, but an "attitude" problem. He noted, "You go into a neighborhood on a complaint, and if you didn't have an address you could find nine out of ten by looking at their yards. It's an attitude issue, not necessarily a money issue." Another officer pointed out: "Often we'll go to the house and the house can be gorgeous. And you say to yourself, 'Okay, everything is going to be fine.' And usually it's going to be. But you come to a house and the screens are ripped, the windows are missing, you know that you're going to have a problem."

Before officers knocked on doors, they examined the surrounding property because animals might be outside and easily seen from the street or sidewalk. Some officers ventured down respondents' driveways and into their yards to better observe animals and how they were kept. "I'll walk around the house to see if I can see something before I get shut down or sort of see what the hell the situation is, and then knock on the door." By doing this, they also learned about the condition of animals inside homes. For example, in one case of a dog allegedly being "kept in a closet all day," the officer could hear the dog barking from outside the house and felt confident that it was not in the closet, at least at that time. As another officer said, this preliminary checking paid off if respondents refused to cooperate: "If it's something like a dog being kept in a cellar and you can find a window, you know—'thin dog kept in cellar'—and the person owns the house and they don't show it to you, then it's like, 'What is going on?' They could not be showing you because they feel 'You're not going to violate my rights,' but usually I think it's because something's going on and they know that there's something wrong down there."

In rare cases, if respondents were not there, officers conducted improper searches and entered homes because they were "concerned" about animals thought to be in danger. This was not done casually or without good reason. "That fact that you are concerned about the animals means that sometimes you end up doing things which would be considered an illegal search," admitted one officer. Another explained why he walked into an unlocked apartment:

> You know, every time I entered that apartment, I not only conducted an illegal search, but entered the apartment illegally. The fact that the door doesn't latch and everything came into play there too, in that anybody could enter the apartment. Not that that gives you an excuse, but if I present it because, "Yeah, I went in there because I was concerned based on what I had been told." And I felt that the people [neighbors] were forthcoming. If the people were vague, if they said, "I'm not sure if there was food down for the animals," or "I'm not sure about this or that," then I may not have entered the apartment right away. I may have given it a day or two before I went in. So it's hard to have a steadfast rule—say, this type of complaint is going to be handled every single time because it doesn't work that way because there's so many different variables that come into play there. Say a situation where someone said, "I entered the apartment and the dog is on a chain and it's lying there and it's lethargic and it looks like it's dying," what are you going to do? Tape the doors and go back in two days and say, "Oh, yeah, I guess it looked like it was dying because it's dead now."

More routinely, respondents invited officers into their homes to talk about complaints and to allow observation of animals. Entry into respondents' homes often proved to be invaluable. Even a quick look behind a front door sometimes revealed how an animal was being treated. For instance, when investigating a complaint of a dog "never taken out, unsanitary conditions," an eight-year-old child answered the door because he was home alone. Although the officer could not enter the home, she did get a quick look at the dog and the house, concluding: "The dog looked okay. I didn't smell a real strong odor coming out. There wasn't feces all over the kitchen door. The dog seemed like he had run of the house because the minute I knocked he came to the side door. He doesn't seem tied or anything."

The condition of the home's interior also told officers about the quality of care given animals. Many remembered being disgusted by noxious smells and utter chaos. Dirty and disorderly interiors did not surprise officers, who saw this as an expression of a general attitude of neglect or indifference toward animals. As one officer remarked, "Sometimes you go in these places and it makes you wonder how these people can live. Cockroaches and . . . It's the typical out of work, sitting in his chair, drinking beer, watching TV, in a slump, person. He just doesn't care if he is dirty. There's a dog . . ." By noting "there's a dog," the officer was saying that this respondent regarded his animal with the same indifference as he did the rest of his life. These visits shaped officers' expectations of respondents and how well, or not, they cared for animals. One staff member contrasted working with respondents who lived in clean, orderly homes:

> You look at that yard today. It was pretty well picked up. I looked in the house. The house was immaculate inside. There were no dishes or rubbish. So probably the guy and his wife both work until four thirty or five at night. So probably when you talk to them, they'll do what they have to do to straighten the thing out or find a home for the dog, if they really don't want the dog. You go into some houses where, you know, the kids are running around filthy, the house is filthy. They have no money. Probably you're not going to be able to work with them at all. It's going to be, "You do it—either get rid of the dog or you go to court." How they live—it's their general attitude. If someone lives as bad as the animals you're trying to improve, you're not going to improve the care of how the animals are living.

Forming gut impressions also depended on how respondents behaved toward officers. They were never sure what would happen or who would greet them. As one officer said, "You don't know what you're going to see. You can go there for a situation and then find something totally unrelated." Another officer said of respondents in general, "Nothing surprises me anymore. A lot of people that I deal with are almost mentally challenged because they are so far out—extreme and eccentric." Depending on how respondents behaved, officers made certain assumptions about how they treated their animals. For example, one officer said, "I tend to see people sometimes with a violent temper. And I say to myself, 'If this guy is flipping out on me, yelling and screaming, of course he's going to kick his dog.' No doubt in my mind."

"Simple" conversations with respondents were important for officers to consider. They often heard a lot about respondents' lives and problems, although this did not always relate to animal complaints. In fact, officers could feel trapped by respondents who tried to tell them their life stories. "Sometimes you can't get out," one complained. "Sometimes somebody will call you in and you can't get out of the house. They want to tell you their life story." In one case, the officer was investigating a complaint of sheep with overgrown hooves. When the respondent was approached, she told the officer, "'I just got out of the hospital and I have heart problems, so you can't upset me.' After a couple of minutes I got her whole life story. She and her husband just broke up and she hasn't taken care of the animals at all because she's having such emotional problems. I mean, these feet didn't get to be that way when her problems started, so it's not an excuse." But some of these conversations were revealing. Officers heard things suggesting that animals were not well cared for by respondents. In one such case, a respondent told an officer a lengthy story of her marital discord, revealing that she was given a puppy—the animal named in the complaint—as a birthday present that she did not want.

Officers noticed how respondents answered questions about their animals or responded to investigations. For example, one respondent appeared to be "bent out of shape" or noticeably disturbed after being accused of starving her Great Dane. At one point, the officer asked her what veterinarian she used, and she quickly replied with his name, location, and the date of her last visit. This impressed the officer and made him think that she was a responsible pet owner, in addition to the fact that the dog was not thin. He commented about reading responses to his questions, "A lot of times during the conversation, I solicit stuff out of people without asking them direct questions. 'Who's the vet you use?' 'I can't remember his name.' 'When was the last time it was at a vet?' 'I can't remember.' At that point I'm going to check with the vet because you're not totally sure whether they have had their animal to a vet or not. But you get someone who throws out, 'Oh, yes, Smith Veterinary Clinic, a couple of weeks ago. I remember because it was the week before I went on vacation.' Stuff like that, you know the chances are they're not lying." In another case, a dog was allegedly kept outside all night without shelter during winter. The investigating officer believed the respondent after briefly talking with her and seeing the dog. He trusted her words when she said, "The dog is the love of our lives. He's spoiled rotten," and believed her when she said that the complainant was harassing her, given additional information he collected about the source of the complaint. The officer also did not see her violating the law, since tying a dog outside was a violation only if done for extended periods without shelter. Commenting about such cases, the officer reflected: "When they do have the dogs out, they either will lie to you or . . . but I'll have somebody that's genuinely concerned. I don't know . . . it's just one of those things you just feel. I don't think the dog was out all the time. He might be out for a couple of hours a day, but I don't think he's out if it's bad weather. She showed me where he goes. He goes into the kitchen or the basement. He's never out at night." In such instances, gut impressions led officers to trust respondents.

Talking with respondents sometimes made officers distrust their reports and suspect that animals were in fact mistreated. They caught some in their lies during inspections of animals and their surroundings. This happened with one respondent accused of keeping her dog in unsanitary conditions. When the officer arrived at her home, the respondent claimed that she hosed down the floor of her dog's cage once an hour. However, examination of the cage revealed fecal matter on its floor, leading the officer to conclude, "So you know she's lying about that."

If they continued to be suspicious, officers sometimes made unannounced, repeat visits to catch respondents. One officer described how he might try to do this with a respondent suspected of keeping his dog outside on very hot summer days without any shelter. He claimed, "If I get a day where it's slow or I don't have a lot of complaints, I may swing by and check to see if that dog is out. And if it's out, I'll go knock on the door and say, 'Geez, I just happened to be going by and I noted your dog is out.' Or I might swing by and leave and do a couple of other things and come back in an hour and see if the dog is out. And I'll say to him, 'Geez, I noted the dog is out.' That person, in most cases, is going to say, 'I just put the animal out.' And I'll say, 'You know, I hate to differ with you, but I went by an hour ago and the dog was out.'" Catching respondents could take more work than driving by their homes and observing their animals. For example, an officer talked about how he might try to catch someone who allegedly abandoned his animals. "What you do is you go there and, if someone's not home, then you scotch tape the doors. Come back the next day and see if the tape is broken. If the tape is broken, you know someone is coming and going through the apartment. If the tape is not broken, then you know no one has gained access to that apartment through doors, as far as that's concerned. So it starts to establish probable cause that there may be a problem there." Catching respondents through such mundane tactics as taping doors or driving by homes allowed officers to confirm gut impressions that animals were indeed mistreated.

More important than assessing talk, forming gut impressions depended on officers' directly observing animals and their surroundings as they looked for obvious signs of care or lack thereof, such as the presence of food and water. They felt that some respondents tried to disprove complaints by showing them their animals, as if doing this was itself evidence of their proper treatment. In one case of an alleged dog without shelter, the respondent asked the officer if she wanted to see the animal, as though seeing the dog would convince the officer that it was not outside at night without shelter. As she noted, "I said, 'They called us about shelter.' And then she said, 'You want to see my dog?' And I said, 'Yeah, I'd like to see the dog.' When people purposely bring you their animal and say, 'Doesn't he look fine?' I say, 'The dog looks fine, but that's not why I'm here. The question was about shelter.'"

Techniques to form gut impressions were the bricolage of animal police, assembled from their on-the-job experience in the field and in the department. Like the handyman or jack of all trades (Harper 1987) who adapts available material to repair or build things, officers utilized the knowledge they collected from investigating cruelty and from talking to colleagues. They improvised the odds and ends presented in the details of cases and discovered when observing respondents and animals. Their stock of techniques to read cases for these odds and ends enlarged through practice. They were the invented tools of the trade that distinguished the seasoned officer from the rookie. Such improvisation gave officers a sense of control, if not mastery, over situations that were extremely vague and uncertain. In the end, this control relied on the creative use of ideas and techniques built up during the process of investigating cruelty.

Although the process of telling the story of abuse and creating an impression of abusers was rarely a simple matter, officers made enough sense of ambiguous complaints to form a picture in their minds of respondents and their animals. They trusted their gut feelings about how much respondents cared for their animals and whether they were intentionally cruel, and felt confident that they understood how much animals suffered and why they did so. Yet putting together these stories could leave officers uneasy or deeply upset. Rookies were emotionally vulnerable when witnessing the mistreatment of animals, although more experienced staff members, especially those who were animal-inclined, also could be disturbed by the occasional bad case. Over time, however, most officers developed ways of approaching difficult investigations that buffered the emotional cost of telling the animal's story.

Bracketing Cruelty

Cases could leave officers troubled, especially when they involved graphic and deplorable acts of cruelty. Rookies in particular found these gruesome cases very distressing to consider; as one said, "I see all these horrific things and it's like, nobody's going to believe me. I knew stuff like that happened, but I never saw it before. And it's different when you take the call in the office and hear the person say they're doing this or that, but you don't visualize it. You don't see the living and breathing dog or cat or horse going through it. It's totally different when it's a live animal in front of you and not just someone talking." In the course of their investigations, every

This cat was burned to death. Such egregious cases of cruelty shock even seasoned officers.

officer at some point got the egregious case—the cat crucified or set on fire, the horse neglected to the point where its overgrown hooves prevented it from stand-

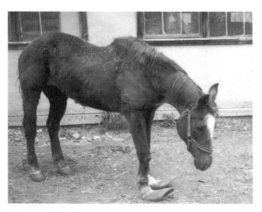

This horses's owner has neglected the animal. It is very thin, and its hooves have been allowed to grow, making it difficult for the animal to walk.

ing. And in the course of their work, virtually all officers felt shaken, even sickened, by what they saw, forcing them to put aside or rethink their emotions just enough to continue.

Officers were puzzled and even shocked when they compared their own treatment of animals to that of respondents. In one instance, an officer investigated a case of an extremely thin dog—a sixty-pound Rottweiler—that should have weighed about one hundred pounds. "The dog was skin and bones, so weak he couldn't even get up. The person told me he was minding the dog for his son because his son had been away. He'd go out every night at 5:00 and dump food on the ground, and because it was dark, he really couldn't see if the dog was thin. That was his excuse." The officer told the respondent, "Listen, it is your house. You agreed to care for the dog." He even spoke with the son, who said his father had been caring for the dog. So the respondent surrendered the dog and it was euthanized by a veterinarian. "It was too far gone. We had to carry it on a stretcher. It was unbelievable. It really was bad. The dog also had a large abscess on its left ear that looked like it was infected. So I charged him with animal cruelty—failure to provide necessary sustenance." This officer contrasted the respondent's treatment of the dog to how he and his wife treated their dog: "I get upset. It bothers me that somebody would do that to an animal because my wife and I have a black Lab and we love her. She is part of our family. We can't comprehend something like that. It's difficult." Another officer, after investigating a complaint of inadequate shelter, regretted that the dog was being kept in minimally acceptable conditions—an overturned barrel for shelter, a dirty bucket of water to drink, and a very short chain. She said of the case, "That was sad. You realize how lucky the pets that you have or your friends have are. That dog has a hell of a life."

Respondents' reactions in these cases could be almost as disturbing as the abuse itself. Officers were confused and unnerved by the occasional respondents who appeared to have strong, positive feelings for their animals, despite their neglect or cruelty. These cases baffled officers because they could not understand how respondents could mistreat animals they also professed to love. An officer described just such a respondent's reaction to the seizure of her animals: "She was sad, very sad, when I talked to her that morning [the day her animal was removed]. She started crying. She loved the horse, but I can't understand how somebody can love an animal and not give it proper care." In rare but disturbing incidents of violence, respondents expressed love for animals that had been seriously or fatally harmed. In a case where a respondent allegedly beat his dog to death, the investigating officer said, "Why would somebody do that? It's amazing. He had the dog for thirteen years. I saw pictures of the dog. He obviously loved the dog. The picture said, 'Tom's best friend, Blackie.' He had pictures everywhere in his house. It's disturbing. The dog wasn't doing anything." Paradoxical cases such as these were rare.

More commonly, respondents in egregious cases denied harming their animals and showed little affect. These reactions deeply affected rookies, at least in the short term. For instance, when one of the younger officers investigated a complaint involving the improper care of cows, he discovered a grisly scene of death and suffering that greatly disturbed and angered him, including a starving calf standing in foot-thick feces alongside of several dead, maggot-covered cows. The respondent's reaction further angered the officer; he was only upset because the dead cows cost him money. To the farmer, the cows were just "milk or meat machines," observed the officer. Although the incident did not shock a senior officer involved in the case, it had that impact on the distressed rookie. He reported "losing a lot of sleep" over this cruelty. "It was the worst I've seen." So angered by what he saw, the junior officer launched a determined effort to build the strongest court case possible, including taking numerous photographs of the barn scene to illustrate the extent of cruelty. "I am going way overboard to build a strong case," he said, adding, "this has affected me in a personal way." The officer claimed that the impact of witnessing this scene was so great, he became a vegetarian. He also hung a photograph of the calf on his refrigerator door, so that he would never be tempted to eat meat again.

Over time, most officers "hardened" themselves to the suffering of animals and the inappropriateness of their owners, although animal-inclined agents found it harder to do this than did their police-oriented peers. They certainly were not alone in making such an adjustment. Professionals in other fields who routinely deal with disturbing situations, such as emergency medical technicians (Metz 1981), go through a similar transformation as they learn to control their thinking and feeling. In this regard, several officers spoke about their hardening. As one said, "I think I've become a little more hardened, a little less sensitive to some things. Not that I think that I don't do my job properly. I just don't get as worked up over things as quickly as I used to when I first started out." To be hardened, officers learned to "not think" about troubling cases. They bracketed cruelty. One officer briefly put it, "So if something bothers me, I try not to think about it. I try not to think about how the dog, or whatever animal, had to suffer. I just kind of look at it as something I have to do."

Although officers bracketed cruelty, controlling their thinking and feeling did not mean that they became completely blunted. Rather than being shocked by what they saw, officers diminished, but did not erase, their emotional reactions. They still evidenced concern, reminding them that at least some humane sensitivity remained. As one explained, "You find a lot of animals in bad shape, but when you first get into the job and you see something that's a little thing, you say, 'Oh, my goodness, they've got to feed that.' And as you see more and more animals in poorer and poorer shape, you get, not desensitized to it, but the shock isn't there when you go there and see a dog with all its ribs showing and yet he's alert and bouncing around." Seasoned officers still encountered "bad" cases that broke through their hardened feelings, but this happened infrequently compared to rookies because their perspectives were different. From the former's view, it was "very rare that you find an animal that's on the last legs," while for the latter more animals seemed to be on their "last legs." And when encountering such distressed animals, seasoned officers, especially those having a police-orientation, were less likely to view their condition with the same urgency or seriousness as rookies or those having an animal inclination. "When you first come on, if you saw something bad, you're all excited, and then after thirty years, you see so many bad things, you become a little hardened. It doesn't bother you as much because you see so many animals in poor condition."

Officers realized that a fine line existed between maintaining some humane sensitivity and losing it all. Complete desensitization was generally regarded as a bad thing, especially among animal-inclined members of the department. One officer commented about the dangers of this happening: "You could get yourself to the point where you aren't sensitive enough if you're not careful. You start to discount everything and you start to become very cynical about what everybody tells you." Aware of and concerned about his own hardening, another officer said that talking to his wife helped him not to "minimize" cases. In his words, "Sometimes you have to sit there and keep reassessing yourself. From time to time I sit there and explain things to my wife or I'll show pictures to her and I'll say, 'What do you think of this?' I'll try to get a different perspective on it because you see so many things that are extreme, sometimes you start minimizing some of the stuff. So it's helpful to get another perspective on things." Many other officers tuned into their own declining sensitivities and improvised various techniques for recharging them, including talking to others in the department, working closely with rookies, or recalling disturbing investigations. The latter cases were recalled in different ways. Although unusual, one officer kept a small album in his police car of pictures showing the dirtied and chaotic interior of an animal hoarder's house, a case he dealt with years earlier. Another had hundreds of photos at home of severely abused animals that he investigated over the years. Originally taken as "evidence" to be shown in court, should the investigations go that far, he kept the photos as "reminders" of prior cases.

Learning to not dwell on cruelty enabled officers to cope with cases of abuse that might otherwise disturb them. They bracketed cruelty, or put it aside in their minds, just enough to stop it from taking over their emotions. However, sometimes officers faced more immediate problems. For their own safety, they had to read situations to protect themselves from both animals and people.

Suspending Trust

Investigations were not only ambiguous, but potentially dangerous. Animals and people could pose trouble. Officers needed a suspicious or critical mindset to safely tell the animal's story. Until proven otherwise, they proceeded with a what-if assumption, assuming that danger could present itself in any situation despite appearances to the contrary. This foreign, if not uncomfortable, attitude repressed officers' everyday expectations about animals and respondents. The former could not be played with as pets, and the latter could not be socialized with as friends.

Dealing with Animals

While animals rarely attacked officers during investigations, they could bite, scratch, stomp, or kick them. To some extent, these mishaps were unpredictable. Odd events or accidents created danger in otherwise safe situations. One officer, for instance, walked into a stable and the respondent was on the phone. Waiting for her, he patted and talked to a horse. Because she did not see the officer enter the stable, the respondent was startled and screamed when she got off the phone and saw him. Her screams provoked one of the dogs in the stable to attack him. She continued to scream and a second dog attacked the officer, who asked the respondent to stop yelling and call off her dogs. In his words, "I kind of threw myself against the stall, and I had my hands in the air. One had me by the side. One had my wallet. Another one had my hand. They were all over me. So she finally got the one big dog off and the other ones just let go once the big one was off. He had me right by the side here, so all my muscles . . . I couldn't even move afterwards. I went to the hospital and they gave me shots. So it's like now, when I go to that stable, I drive in and I won't get out until I know where that dog is. And then you are like, 'Oh, I better be a little bit more careful.'" For self-protection the officer altered his future behavior at this particular stable. Nevertheless, a certain amount of risk is built into the job and cannot be eliminated.

To reduce this risk, officers temporarily put aside their strong positive feelings for animals and relied on a different attitude on the job. Rather than "trusting" animals being investigated, as officers did with everyday pets, they became wary of them and their owners. Adopting this attitude was counterintuitive, especially for rookies who usually trusted animals they met. Yet rookies quickly learned that animals could be dangerous. One newcomer's assumptions about animals incorrectly led her to approach a dog as though it were her own. She admitted, "Sometimes I put more trust in the animal than I should. Especially around Pit Bulls and stuff because I'm a Pit Bull person and I think they are all like mine. I'll just go up and get right near it and then have him growling at me." She investigated a complaint of "a very skinny dog running loose." In her words, "Right there it should be a red flag that the dog's loose. But I'm thickheaded and I started walking up and all of a sudden the dog sticks his head out of the porch. He was about a hundred and twenty-pound Mastiff. He was just kind of looking at me a little bit. I wasn't worried about it. And he came over and he greeted me and I petted him a little bit, and then I turned around and got bit in the butt, which dogs like to do." Rookies learned not to trust animals after getting "burned." As one said, "You get growled at, you get charged. I haven't been doing this that long, but I've already run out of a few backyards because I didn't know how long the chain was. You know, you got this big Cujo coming at you."

Despite their weariness, officers approached animals when situations appeared to be safe. They developed this confidence in several ways. First, they looked for clues in the animal's behavior that suggested possible aggressiveness. When certain danger signs appeared, officers stopped interacting with them in an everyday fashion. As one officer explained this strategy, "Certain signs, like obvious signs of territory. Like the Husky we saw this morning. That dog had an obvious area of territory there. You noticed I didn't go running right up to the dog. I was sitting there talking to it and once the dog started wagging its tail and showing signs that it wasn't going to be aggressive, then I started walking up to the dog, and even then, I didn't get right up to the dog's face." Certain sounds made by animals were another signal alerting officers to danger. Although they may not act aggressively, dogs have a muted growl that can indicate an attack or bite is possible. When such clues were absent, officers proceeded to interact with animals assumed to be safe.

A second way they developed confidence in animals was to watch how they interacted with respondents or others present. One officer investigated a no-shelter, no-water complaint and walked down the respondent's driveway to look at the dog tied up in the backyard. While respecting the dog's territory, he observed its behavior around the respondent. Signals indicated a safe animal: "The dog looked okay. This dog was giving body language that it was going to be friendly. Once he [the owner] came out there, you could see that the dog was showing signs that it was friendly. If the guy isn't home, a lot of times I'll walk into a backyard to look at the situation, but I'm very careful at that point." However, when reading these human-animal interactions, officers sometimes got signals that spurred precautions. For example, when dogs tried to protect owners, officers moved back quickly from the area. For another, if owners changed their tone of voice in the presence of a dog, it might prompt the latter to attack officers. One officer gave an example of this: "If a woman started to get irritated with me and started to raise her voice, her dog might turn around and nail me because she changed the tone of her voice. You have to read the owner. You have to be able to realize that you're far enough back that if this woman starts to get upset and the dog starts to really growl or make a lunge for you, you can get back far enough where the dog is not a problem."

A third way to build confidence required officers to critically listen to the reports of respondents about their animals' behavior. There might be reassurances that animals were safe to approach, inspect, and touch, but officers had to decide whether to question these words. One officer had a call where the dog appeared to be threatening, despite the respondent's opinion to the contrary. The complaint was about a Boxer allegedly in the sun with no shelter. When the officer arrived she saw a Pit Bull on the porch. She whistled to it, but the dog would not get up. As the officer approached the front stairs, she took out her OC [mace] and had it in her hand. She knocked on the door and the respondent came to the door. The dog started to get up. She said to the woman, "How is the dog?" The respondent said, "Oh, the dog is friendly." As the officer talked to her, she watched the dog, asking, "Are you sure?" because "when the dog got up he had his head down, he had his ears drooped, he had his tail between his legs, which all indicates an unhappy camper." The respondent replied, "Yeah." The dog started walking toward the officer and got within a few feet when suddenly the dog started to growl and lunged for her. "If I wasn't keeping an eye on the dog, he would have got me right on the side of the neck because when he hit me, he hit me right in the shoulder area." She pushed him from the chest backwards and sprayed his face with the mace. In another case, a Chow attacked an officer after reassurance by the owner that the dog would be safe to approach. The officer described what happened on this no-shelter complaint, "I had a close call. I did see the dog out back in the dog house, and I went back to speak to them and they said, 'The dog's friendly, don't worry about it.' And I went back, but I was cautious. I had my clip board. Geez, the dog tried to tear my head off. I held my clipboard out and the dog jumped at that and tried to bite the clipboard." Officers also distrusted signs put up by respondents claiming that animals could be safely approached. As one said, "Animals in fenced in areas—yeah, it's in a fenced in area—is the fence adequate to keep the animal? When I go around a corner of a house, I always take a wide turn because that way you get to see what's around the corner without getting faced with something because it says 'dog in pen,' but I've been to places before where 'dog in a pen' is actually a dog on a leash."

Incorrectly reading animals, or clues about them from respondents, could be dangerous. If misjudged, dogs in particular could badly hurt attacked officers. A dilemma resulted. Although they had a license to shoot, if endangered, many factors argued against the use of deadly force. Of course, using this option occurred to officers, but very few ever fired their weapons. For example, one officer on a no-shelter call found a threatening Pit Bull in a small cage; she considered using her gun but did not: "This fifty-pound Pit Bull was rocking it, and we're trying to tell the lady, 'Put your hand on that and steady that cage. I'm not getting bitten by that dog.' She couldn't even put her hand on it, the dog was so excited. He was biting her. And if that dog got out, mace wouldn't have stopped that dog, and I would have had to have shot the dog."

Officers avoided using force for several reasons. They had high regard for animals and would rather not hurt them, even if attacked, especially when the aggressiveness was apparently caused by their owner's treatment. Indeed, many officers were apprehensive about shooting animals because they received little specific training to do this and felt inexperienced. They particularly feared a situation where the first shot did not kill an animal, forcing them to fire additional shots. A newcomer gave the example of shooting a horse, although the animal did not pose a danger to her. She said: "You aren't trained on exactly where you should shoot an animal. I mean, there are books and stuff, like where to get a horse. But they don't tell you what happens when the animal flinches and you're off by a quarter of a centimeter and the animal starts flailing."

Another reason why officers refrained from shooting was their concern about being sued and losing. If they ended up in court, it would only be their "word" against the respondent's. Because of this, most believed that it was wiser to withdraw from danger than to shoot an animal. In one such encounter, an officer was standing in the doorway talking to the respondent with his dog. The respondent said, "What if I turn this dog loose on you?" Later, the officer recounted, "So right away, I knew what I was dealing with. The police told me this guy was a real character, so be careful of him." In reply, the officer said, "Well, I'm going to tell you right now, if you let him loose, I'm going to shoot the son of a bitch." The respondent then said, "You can't shoot him, you're an MSPCA officer," to which the officer replied, "Let me tell you something right now. If you value your dog, you will hang on to him and you won't give him any commands because I'm going to shoot him. I have the right to protect myself and that includes you, so if you don't want to get placed under arrest, put the dog inside." Reflecting on what happened, the officer said that if the Pit Bull were released to attack him, shooting it would have been a mistake. "You have to know when to turn around and leave. You have to know when to stop the conversation, get into your car and leave. If you get into a confrontation, it's your word against that person's word, so you've got to remember you are on his property. If he says that you went for his neck, it's your word against his. The best thing you can do at that point is to vacate."

A final constraint on officers' use of force was their concern for damaging or compromising the public image of the humane society and its law enforcement department. For instance, one officer took the precaution of blowing his car horn to see if an untied dog might charge him if he approached the respondent's house. He spoke about why such precautions were necessary to avoid personal injury and the use of weapons: "Like I will pull up to a house sometimes and honk the horn a couple of times to see if a dog is going to come running because you don't know. Everybody says, 'Oh, don't worry about it, you carry mace, you've got a gun.' And I say, 'I realize that, but you gotta remember you are the MSPCA—you are preventing cruelty to animals.'" Another officer acknowledged the department's unofficial "policy" not to shoot animals, while explaining his approach in a potentially dangerous situation. He spoke about being hesitant to use force when walking toward a respondent's front door and seeing a large dog barking in a threatening manner. When asked what he was thinking at the time, the officer replied, "Is he [the dog] going to go through the screen? And if he does, what do I do? I do have a gun. Do I shoot him? The MSPCA doesn't have a policy on that. If you did shoot like that, there would be criticism because you're supposed to be protecting them. It would be a publicity nightmare."

Dealing with People

Despite problems posed by animals, officers agreed that the most difficult and dangerous aspect of their work came from people they encountered on the job. As one officer admitted, "The animals are easy to deal with. It's the two-legged animals that you have the problems with. People say to me, 'Oh, you get to work with animals all day.' I say, 'Yeah, I do—four-legged animals and two-legged animals. And the two-legged animals are the problem.'" Most thought that people were more unpredictable than animals and therefore harder to read. "I would consider the animal dangers minimal [compared] to some of the human dangers. The animal dangers, you realize they are there, and in most cases you are trained enough to deal with the situation, to read the situation properly. You accept the animal dangers. It's the human dangers that are unpredictable. People can snap like that. They turn like that," explained one officer. This unpredictability could take many dangerous forms, but at its core was the "riled" respondent. As one officer explained, "If you get somebody that gets riled, they are going to lunge for you. The chances are that it's not going to happen. But if you approach a person the wrong way and get them riled, he could run for you." And riled respondents might be armed.

Mistaken authority could "rile" respondents. Striking out at officers might be a reaction to all their trappings of authority—the badges, uniforms, guns, and official car. They were unwelcome and unknown law enforcement figures knocking on respondents' doors and might appear, at first, to be regular police. As one officer pointed out, "People see someone coming up to their house with a uniform on and they got a warrant. They don't look to see if it says MSPCA or state police or such and such security. It's a uniform." The official-looking uniform and badge threatened some respondents and made them attack officers. "Some of these people come to the door like they are going to blow your head off," commented an officer. He continued, "You could be knocking on somebody's door and they could be doing something illegal and when they see the uniform, not knowing who you work for, they could panic and do something stupid." "Something stupid" could include being shot at by an "irrational" respondent who "flips out."

Some respondents became riled because they mistook humane agents for animal control officers encountered before because of prior animal problems. Respondents, at these times, became very annoyed because they felt harassed. An officer described such a situation: "We were standing in the barn talking to this one kid for quite a while, and then his partner comes out and starts ranting and raving. He was so ticked off that we were there. We were like, 'What's your problem?' It turned out that somebody was there, not too long ago, but it wasn't us. It's like, just because you see a person, it does not mean it's the MSPCA."

Once officers identified themselves as humane law enforcement agents, respondents could still be riled. Seemingly annoyed by officers and unimpressed by their authority, some respondents angrily dismissed them. One gave the following example of such an encounter, "After I said who I was and why I was there, this guy slammed the door at me and I threw my foot in the door. Then he wanted my card. I gave him my card and he crinkled it up and said, 'Screw it.' And it went down the landing. Then he wanted my name. I said, 'You want my name? Haul your ass out and you go down to the landing where you threw my card. Then you'll know who I am.' And I told him what I was there for, what I wanted, I warned him, and I left."

Others became upset because they feared that officers would take their animals away from them. Fueling their fear was the mistaken assumption that officers could easily seize their animals, although doing this was actually quite difficult. For example, during an investigation of a complaint about a dog and puppies without water, two pre-adolescent boys asked the officer if their puppies would be taken away and gestured hostilely toward the officer, despite his reassurance to the contrary. The officer said of this incident, "They probably figured I was coming to take them. You're always the jerk." And other respondents became upset because they feared prosecution, which, like seizure, was far more difficult to do than generally thought. In one case, a respondent allegedly killed his cat but would not tell officers what happened to it. When the investigating officer hinted at possible prosecution, the respondent become noticeably alarmed, assumed a threatening pose, and started shouting profanities.

Respondents also became riled when officers arrived at the "wrong place at the wrong time." For instance, they could step into ongoing disputes between respondents and spouses, children, or neighbors. An officer spoke about one of his own cases where this occurred: "People are fighting in front of you. Like the one that I just had now, the husband and wife are feuding. I was concerned that he'd [husband] come out of the house with a shotgun or something." Officers also could encounter riled and dangerous respondents when breaking up their private, and sometimes illegal, activities. For example, on his way into a "real low-grade apartment building," one officer was concerned that "drunks sleeping inside" the lobby could become threatening. Dog- or cockfighting raids were also considered dangerous to investigate. An officer described what happened to him during one such raid when he went in alone: "I had my gun out. And in the back of my head, I'm saying 'I'm going to shoot somebody for this shit.' So I put the gun away. In fact, I didn't even put it in the holster. I put it in my jacket because I was worried that they would take my gun. And I talked my way out, but on the way out, once I got in the yard, they were throwing stones at me . . . the whole bit. I just backed off and the next day we went in and removed the animals."

If not angry at officers, respondents became riled with complainants for reporting them to the authorities. In fact, they often became more concerned about identifying the complainant than they were about the charge of cruelty. As one officer said, "Most people don't care about the animal thing, even where there are blatant violations. It's, 'Who's messing with me? I don't beat my dog. Who's saying I beat my dog? I want to know who called. It's my God-given right to know who called about me. This is America!' They never say, 'Oh yeah, I beat my dog.' Then they're angry at you for coming." Typically, respondents were sure that they knew who filed complaints against them. An officer elaborated, "They [respondents] always accuse somebody of doing this [making the complaint]. 'It has to be them. It has to be them.'" In some cases, they were right. "A lot of people will ask about the complainant. The funny part about it is that it's not at all unusual for someone to say, 'Well, I think it's so-and-so over there—Mary Jones—' and a lot of times they are correct because they've had dealings before with the people over this animal issue," said one officer.

When agitated respondents were not sure, they frequently pressured officers to identify the source of the complaint. In one case, an officer felt worn down by this pressure: "He kept saying, 'Come on, just give me a name, give me the name.' He was tugging, and I came as close to giving a name out as I ever came. But I didn't." Officers feared that if respondents knew or thought they knew who lodged complaints against them they would have bitter confrontations with complainants. An officer warned about such hostilities and not getting in between respondents who were confronting complainants. "The next thing you know, they're going at it. And I'm trying to tell the respondent, 'If you don't go back to your house, I'm leaving. You can fight between you, but I'm not going to sit here and try to resolve this.' When that happens, you don't get anything done. It becomes a big feud. And now, because they know who the complainant is, they are not going to do anything for you. It becomes like a Jerry Springer show."

Officers improvised various strategies to curtail the pressure to name complainants and to calm down respondents. One tactic was to remind them that the Attorney General prohibited complainant's names from becoming public record. Another tactic was for officers to tell inquiring respondents that the callers were anonymous or unknown, making it possible to mask the identities of complainants. "If I have a complainant and someone asks me who it is, I'll say I don't know. Why stir up things . . . what's the point? If you say, 'I know, but I can't tell you,' then you're just opening yourself up to a whole can of worms. And the poor animal is left by the wayside. You never get done what you want to get done." A final strategy was to create false identities: "I'll tell people a fictitious name, maybe somebody from work, just to shut them up. But most of the time, I tell them it's anonymous, even if I know who it was, so they don't keep pushing the issue. Or I'll say, 'Look, I know who complained. I can't tell you, but I'll tell you it wasn't your neighbor because I spoke to the person. Somebody was driving by and happened to see it.' And all the time I know it was the neighbor." These strategies enabled officers to maintain control of situations that otherwise could degenerate into heated discussions about complainants instead of dealing with cruelty complaints themselves.

Officers also adopted various working personalities to calm down respondents in general, whatever the cause, as do regular police (Skolnick 1994). One, for instance, took the nice-guy approach: "When I go and talk to people, I tell them who I am and I tell them why I'm there. But I'm friendly with them. That's how I do complaints because I find that works for me. I walk up like, 'Oh, I'm just Mr. Friendly.' I've had people who I know are on some drug where they wouldn't think twice about slitting my neck. They end up being very friendly to me. They want to shake my hand and slap me on the back." Another officer talked about how he used a polite and reasonable style to "diffuse" angry respondents: "We go to somebody's home and accuse them of animal cruelty. People get very emotional when it involves their animals. If you go in there like you are a hard ass, saying, 'You violated a law, you're going to be in trouble,' they're going to treat you one way. But if you go in there and try to be polite and say, 'I understand that people get upset, but we have a job to do, too,' then they take it differently. They look at you like you're just doing your job." Another officer dissipated strong emotional reactions by being good humored. He described how to handle difficult respondents: "Some get very vocal, very animated. They get to the point where, unless you can calm them down, unless you can get them to stop yelling, you're not going to deal with them because they're just not listening. They're off on their own agenda, trying to yell and scream and carry on. I'll say to them, 'Why are you getting so upset? It's too hot to get upset.' That's the type of thing that I use." And yet another officer calmed down respondents and controlled situations by being a distracting conversationalist. "In some cases you can avoid that too; when you are talking to them about their animals . . . like the woman in Shoretown, 'Oh, yeah, you were on vacation. Where did you go on vacation? Was the weather good?'"

Once the respondent was calmed down, officers believed they could refocus the attention of the respondent on the animal in question. In the words of one staff member, "They don't even care who you are or why you're there. They're never going to get a doghouse. You have to first calm them down and then bring them around to, 'I know your neighbors hate you, not everybody can get along.' So you have to try to bring it back to the dog, so they get a more sympathetic approach." Once their focus was on the animals, officers hoped that respondents could listen to what they were being told and modify their behavior accordingly. "What good is it if I get beat to a pulp? The dog is still going to be in the same situation. I hate losing control. If you're talking to someone about their dog and they are screaming at you, there's no way, unless you get control of the situation back, that they're going to listen to you about what they're going to have to do to fix the dog or change the situation for the dog, if they're not even going to listen to what you have to say," said one officer.

Despite the importance of staying in control, the officers sometimes lost it. When this happened they exited situations, although doing this ran contrary to their training. In one case, an officer advised a screaming and inattentive respondent to keep her dogs out of the sun by using her garage as a shelter. The officer returned to his car rather than continuing to advise her. He noted, "It's hard to walk away because of our training. You're supposed to be in charge and you're supposed to put your point across. But we weren't going to get anything across with that lady. We just were not going to do it. The only thing I could do is mention the garage to her. Maybe, after she calms down and thinks about it, she might do that."

Sometimes they did not exit situations in time to avoid trouble. Despite using various strategies to calm down agitated respondents, they needed to remain alert for possible attack. When respondents became riled, their body language offered important clues to officers about potential attacks, which, if anticipated, might be prevented. One respondent, for example, became very upset because she was being taken to court for allegedly abusing a horse. Her anger and frustration led to inappropriate and threatening contact with an officer. "We were taking her to court and were taking her horses from her. We were removing the horses, and I don't know what she did to me, she put her hand on me and everybody was about to arrest her. But she didn't punch me, but it was obviously an aggressive movement. I was going to mace her, but I didn't." Sometimes violent threats were masked as joking, and officers erred on the safe side by stopping such ambiguous actions, as an officer illustrated, "I had a guy threaten me with a chainsaw. We were serving papers on him and he was cutting wood. I don't know if he was playing or if he wasn't, but he had the thing up and he was walking towards us revving up the engine, that kind of thing. I drew my weapon and told him to put the saw down and he did." Officers quickly dealt with gestures or other acts thought to precede violence. As one said, it was important to set limits on questionable behavior: "I've had cases where people have pushed or shoved me and I deal with that. Right away I tell them, 'Hey, you're getting carried away now, you better back off.' They start getting kind of close to you or start yelling at you and that's when you try to calm them down and let them know you're not going to tolerate their bullshit. At that point, they'll start to mellow out."

Although attacks were rare, officers took precautions in case they occurred. Routine police procedures provided some protection, although officers infrequently used them. For example, some officers wore bulletproof vests, but others felt their work was not dangerous enough to warrant the discomfort of wearing them, except during dog or cockfighting raids. For another form of protection, they exercised good police judgment by doing such things as not letting respondents near them. As one officer said, "I get apprehensive about people being close to you. I get more nervous about being stabbed with a needle or something than I would about being shot." Officers also tried to get backup for riskier cases. Being alone during investigations heightened the need for this precaution, a situation

Breaking up a cockfight involves possible injury—from the animals or from the human participants.

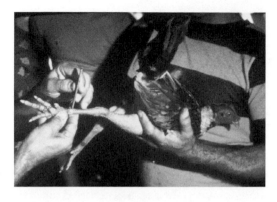

they claimed to face more than regular police officers because the latter were more likely to deal with people on the streets, while animal cops were more likely to deal with them inside their homes. "You're in someone's house and the shit hits the fan, you're by yourself 'cause no one's going to see you at that point." Officers pointed out that respondents inside homes could have weapons, friends and family, and the psychological advantage because the surroundings were familiar.

However, even when danger was anticipated, officers often investigated cases alone due to limited resources. In addition, sometimes they could not get immediate backup because other officers were too far away or could not be reached by radio or phone. At other times, they did not trust that fellow officers would come to their aid, a sentiment shared by regular police (Savitz 1970). Because of this uncertainty, officers would only request backup if they were "comfortable" with the person called; as one explained, "I've gone to places in Badtown that I know I should have backup, but I really don't have anybody any more that I can call right away. Right now, I don't really have anybody that I feel comfortable with and who is available to me. So I've gone to places in Badtown where I know I shouldn't be going by myself, and I know that when police officers go there, there's two or three of them responding to a call." Because they had routine police backup, several officers felt safer conducting cockfighting or dogfighting raids, despite their greater danger, than they did investigating normal cases. One commented, "I feel safer in a raid situation because I wear my vest when I'm in a raid, and because I've got all sorts of people around me. I know if something happens or if I get hurt, at least someone's there to help me out. Under normal circumstances, I got nobody to rely on. So from a safety standpoint, I'm better off in a raid than I am every day." Even having police backup did not guarantee their safety and could actually increase danger: "Sometimes I don't want to get the police to go with me because that comes with a certain amount of baggage that sometimes sets people off when you wouldn't be setting them off. And some police officers you'd rather not have there because of their attitude and the manner in which they deal with situations. So that makes it dangerous."

To be sure, riled respondents rarely erupted into violent behavior and tensions preceding violence usually waned on their own or were diffused quickly and skillfully by officers. Nevertheless, the ever-present risks of investigation reminded officers that they were law enforcers as well as humane workers. Indeed, talk among officers about troublesome respondents and dangerous cases was similar in content and function to "war stories" told by other law enforcers or public authorities. When these attacks occurred they became vital parts of the officers' collective memory and culture about their work. For example, one officer recalled two attacks that happened years earlier: "I had one guy who came at me with a screwdriver. He was a pretty big guy. And then a little kid, like ten, came at me with a knife. If I hadn't seen him and deflected him off I would have been stabbed, but who knows how bad?" In another egregious incident, an officer was attacked by a respondent wielding a club that had also been used to beat cats to death. After a chase on foot, the cornered respondent swung his club at the officer, severely hitting his forehead and causing a serious gash requiring surgical repair. Both stories were part of the culture of the department. Most officers knew about them and retold them to rookies.

Officers had to deal with a great deal of uncertainty when investigating abuse. Assessing the accuracy and seriousness of cruelty complaints involved more than simply observing animals. In many cases, neither animal victims nor respondents revealed enough for officers to definitively conclude that abuse happened. Although animals were carefully examined, officers spent as much or more time reading owners to assess their treatment of animals. Troubles encountered during investigations complicated this process of telling the animal's story. Investigations sometimes posed a risk to officers, distracting them from the task at hand and forcing them to read situations for self-protection. When danger appeared imminent or actually occurred, officers handled it to ensure their safety and to continue their investigations.

However, the fact that respondents could be riled, threatening, or dangerous raises an important question. Once officers deflected such trouble and restored control, how did they create a more humane situation for the animals? As we see in the next chapter, reading respondents for cues of inhumane behavior resulted in narratives about abusers, much like those created by those who work with battered women (Loseke 1992). Officers figured out what kind of person they were dealing with and measured their response accordingly. Based on these narratives, they tried to make respondents into more humane people. How they did so resulted in officers' themselves changing as much or more than did respondents.

4

Brute Force

> When I walked in I wanted to make the arrests. I wanted
> to do good. You know, I wanted to save animals' lives. But
> as time goes on you try to make people aware. Because
> you find out in this job that people are really fucking stu-
> pid. . . . You go from being gung-ho in the beginning to
> seeing the big picture in the long run.

Officers fresh from the academy expected to combat cruelty by taking an aggressive "in your face" approach to getting animals out of "bad situations." Sometimes
this meant pushing respondents to surrender their animals or, if necessary, seizing
them. A rookie gave the following example of how she would push for the surrender of a respondent's animal: "If a dog needs a surgery, like for something
that's going to kill the dog, or something that the dog can die from . . . If it's like a
big open wound and he needs the wound cleaned and closed, then, yeah, you're
going to find a way to bring him to the vet, no matter what, or you're going to
surrender the dog." They also hoped to punish respondents, when necessary and
appropriate. Discussing the above case, the rookie continued, "I'm definitely like,
if they don't bring it to a vet that night, charge them! If my dog needed a twelve-
hundred-dollar surgery, he's getting it."

Rookie aggressiveness even could lead to condemning the respondent's
home in order to get animals out of bad situations. A seasoned officer illustrated
this while training a rookie on a case alleging the under-feeding of cats. The rookie
wanted the cats to be surrendered and the respondent's home to be condemned.

However, the experienced officer insisted that an aggressive approach was wrong, instead suggesting that it would better to give pet food to the respondent so she could feed her cats. "I don't think these people have enough money to feed them all. And they are not in great shape," he said. Although the rookie still wanted to go forward with a surrender, the older officer was firm and asked, "Why don't you try bringing some cat food out there? Help the lady. See if you can get on the good side of her. Maybe we can get somebody to spay and neuter them." In this case that strategy was not enough. The senior officer reported that when the rookie dropped the food off, she said the "lady was running around in her bare feet. There was urine all over the floor. She [the rookie] says the lady had the gas stove on, so she turned around and got the board of health involved and they're going to condemn the place and all that."

As rookies gained more experience, they quickly tempered their enthusiasm in favor of improving situations without punishing respondents or taking their animals from them. They embraced an "educational" approach to resolving complaints, like that used and learned by regular police officers as part of their street or working knowledge (Bayley and Bittner 1984). "I educate people on what they should have done or what to do in the future. But I don't tend to preach to people and say, 'Well, this is your fault. This is 100 percent your fault.' That's not my style. I tend to educate people and say, 'Gee, I know this happened and in the future you have to do this, so it doesn't come out this way again,'" explained one officer. This softer, educational approach was thought to be more practical and effective than the aggressiveness taught at the academy. One experienced officer spoke about how a rookie's approach failed to "get the job done," noting, "At the academy they drum into you that you've got to be this tough officer. So you come out of the academy and you're tough. I think through the years you learn that you really can't get your job done if you continue down that path." Educational skills enabled humane officers to do something if they read respondents and decided that aggressive actions would fail to change their behavior and help animals. They also allowed officers to intervene in situations where respondents were not violating the law but whose animals could use better care.

Coaching

Rather than managing respondents by threatening court, animal seizure, or re-checks, officers learned to deal with them as much or more in the role of teacher than law enforcer. Over time this approach to animal policing made many officers rethink their occupational identity. They felt less like police officers and more like humane educators. As one said, "I don't look at myself anymore as a law enforcement officer. I think of myself as an educator . . . law enforcement is very minor." Another officer estimated that only 10 percent of his job constituted law enforcement work: "Most of what we do isn't really law enforcement. Well it is, but most of the things that we see, we couldn't arrest someone or drive them into court. Most of what we see is just ignorance and just plain not knowing." They dealt with these cases by coaching rather than commanding respondents to change. Their advice, or courtesy teaching, if effective, gently encouraged respondents, who were neither criminal nor cruel, to become more responsible and humane owners of animals.

Getting respondents to understand and carry out their advice required more than passing on raw information or simple suggestions. One strategy was to suggest that caring for animals could "benefit" both animals and the respondents themselves. To illustrate, an officer talked about how he would underscore the value of adding bedding to a doghouse: "You make them think, if they do this, they're going to benefit from it and the animal is going to benefit. I always say, 'I can't make you put straw in there, but you say you love your animal, and I know you want to do the right thing. If you put some straw out there the animal's going to be a lot happier.' You try to make them see that if they do it they are going to be rewarded because the animal is going to reward them." Another strategy was teaching by analogy. In one case, a woman who was the complainant claimed that she could not afford veterinary care for her cat, which a neighbor allegedly injured. The officer pointed out to the woman that she could pay for her children's health care, and that if she did not do the same for her animal, she might become a respondent in the case. He elaborated, "It had an open sore underneath its right leg, like a puncture wound which could have been a bite or could have been a pellet gun. I told her that she had a responsibility as a pet owner to make sure it got treatment. She said she didn't have any money. She couldn't afford it. I said, 'Ma'am, you have to have it treated or else you become the respondent because you have responsibility to take care of it. If this was one of your kids, you couldn't just let it sit here and not do anything. You have to treat it.'" Officers also urged respondents to take the animal's perspective. As one said, "You try and explain to people, 'Look, it would be better for the animal to do this or do that.'" This happened, for example, when respondents refused to euthanize their sick animals, causing unnecessary suffering. Officers recognized that these owners were not deliberately cruel. They needed help making the difficult decision to terminate the lives of their animals. One officer, in fact, felt that his own experience owning pets made it easier for him to "sympathize" with this dilemma. He described how he got respondents to see how euthanasia can be necessary and humane from the animal's perspective, "They sit there and tell you how tough it is, and I tell them I realize that. 'I've been personally involved in it a few times. I know it's not easy. You gotta think of the animal.'" He went on to explain, "It's not unusual for us to get calls and go out some place and find an animal who's in poor condition. Maybe it's just a very old animal and it's getting to the point where it's past time for it. And people don't want to have their animal euthanized. It's sitting there in its own feces or it's sitting there in its own urine, and it's not because the people are trying to be cruel. It's just that they don't want to face the inevitable—that it's time."

Coaching occurred in several situations. For one, officers relied on this strategy when no law was broken but the welfare of animals could be improved. As one said, "You try and explain to people, 'Look, it would be better for the animal to do this or do that.'" An example of trying to improve an animal's quality of life beyond that stipulated by law occurred during an investigation of "unfed dogs." After the officer spoke with the owner and inspected the dogs, he felt that the weight of the animals was acceptable but could have been better. Having worked with these owners before, he knew that the dogs were fed a diet largely consisting of rice. "You try to talk to them and say, 'Well, the dog isn't skinny, but could be much better if you gave it some dog food. No, you don't have to spend a fortune on the best dog food out there, but they really need a little bit more than that.'" Another officer thoughtfully carried straw in his car to urge respondents to buy it for their doghouses. As the officer said, "I carry a bag of straw in the wintertime. I'll say to people, 'I have some in the car.' And they say, 'Oh, that would be great.' And I say, 'Look, go buy a bale. It's only like four dollars, you keep it inside, it will last four or five years because you only use a couple of flakes through the year.'"

Coaching also occurred in "borderline" cases where "some things were not quite right, but not bad enough to seek a complaint." Despite their pessimism, officers hoped to make these respondents more sensitive to the needs of animals. One member of the department gave the example of a complaint concerning a dog that was "tied out [with] no water." The law does not say that the dog has to have water in front of it twenty-four hours a day. It does say that dogs are to be provided with proper food, drink, shelter, or protection from the weather. The officer noted that from a "humane standpoint," it would be beneficial to the animal to have access to water, especially if it were outside for an extended time in the summer. In such cases, the officer explained how he might speak to respondents: "'Gee, it would be better if you're going to be leaving the animal out there for long periods to have water out there for the animal.' Say you get a comment, 'Oh, the animal spills it if I put it out there, so I don't leave water out there.' So then you try and give them a solution as far as how they could secure it, so they're not going to spill it."

Officers coached respondents when there were violations that were not of the "malicious" sort. In many of these cases, informal instruction rather than stern police action seemed warranted. As one officer said, "I have a problem punishing people who I think didn't do something maliciously. I think neglect and maliciousness are so different. It's not like some respondents go out there with a hammer and bash their animals because they bit their flowers or something like that. You can't prosecute everybody that breaks the law." Some respondents, according to officers, were thoughtless, uninformed, or simply lazy when it came to treating their animals. In one case, an owner kept a blanket in his doghouse, apparently unaware or unconcerned that the blanket, once wet, would not quickly dry, especially in the winter. The officer said: "They're lazy and they don't have any idea. You go to their house and most of them have blankets in the dog house. And I say, 'That's no good. Once it gets wet it stays wet. It freezes. You've got to have something like hay or straw that will dry out once the dog lays on it.'" In another case, the respondent seemed unaware of the bad weather and never considered that his pet might prefer a doghouse under such inclement conditions. The officer said:

> I [officer] made myself a complainant because I was driving by and I saw this dog out. There's a dog out there and he was in a pen and going crazy. I left a card and he didn't call me back, so I went, like, four days later. That day it was, like, hailing. So I'm talking to the guy and the dog was outside. And he said, "This dog goes into water that you'd freeze to death in." It was a Spaniel. And I said, "I understand that. I'm sure he likes the weather, but if he wants to get out of the rain, it's his option to do so if he wants to. If he wants to stand in the pouring rain, fine." And the guy is talking to me, and he's like, "Oh, I didn't

know it was raining ice." And I felt like saying, "Bingo, you don't know what it's doing. That's why if you have a doghouse, you don't have to worry about what it's doing." It was definitely one of those "aha" moments. He was one of those "Don't tell me what to do" types and then was like, "Wow, it's pretty bad out here."

Even if it made sense to prosecute because a violation occurred, officers felt that educating was better than going to court in most cases. One talked about how "prosecuting someone is a failure. Success is going over to someone's house for a recheck and seeing the dogs sitting on the couch with the kids. Life is wonderful. I feel, not like a failure, but I feel like the system failed—the bond failed—when I have to prosecute someone. So I judge my success on rechecks, on how the animal is now being treated, and how the quality of life is for the animal." For this reason, respondents were revisited to see if they followed directions, especially in serious complaints. An officer recounted doing this when a complainant drove by a barn and reported sheep in unsanitary conditions. "The barn was beautiful, the cows were perfect, but on the side they have some sheep. They were full of mud and they looked like hell, but they were healthy. But they hadn't been trimmed. It was the middle of winter and he said, 'Well, I'll clip them.' And I said, 'No, you can't clip them down now, it's too cold. Just trim the bottom a little bit, and once you get the bedding in there it will dry up and take care of itself.' I went back and checked it about two weeks ago and it had been all taken care of."

Although officers resorted to coaching respondents, most officers doubted that they could qualitatively change respondents' long-term relationships with animals or make them better owners or guardians. Instead, they took a more practical approach to education, hoping to give some advice that, if followed, improved the well-being of animals in the short term. In one case, the officer investigated a complaint of a "thin dog with no water," only to find a respondent who did not want the dog because it was her cousin's abandoned animal. In addition, the dog recently had given birth to four puppies, which the respondent also did not want. After talking with her, it was clear that she wanted someone to take the dog and its puppies because she had little interest or time to care for them. The officer noticed that the dog was searching for water in the garbage and suggested to the respondent that the dog might be thirsty and that she should provide it with "plenty of water." The puppies, which were scattered around the respondent's yard, appeared close to death and in need of better care. The officer advised the respondent to keep them warm and together so that nursing would be easier. He helped her find a box for the puppies and strongly encouraged her to keep the box inside the house. As she took the box inside, her two young children started to pick up the puppies and roughly play with them, at which point the officer told the respondent not to let her children play with them in this manner. Finally, the respondent asked how she could get rid of the dogs because she was unable to find them a home, to which the officer suggested calling a local veterinary office or shelter for help with this matter. In this case, the officer intervened to temporarily improve the current care of the animals and find a solution to the woman's problem of keeping them. The officer felt satisfied with the woman's response to his suggestions and left not expecting to make return visits to ensure compliance with his advice.

However, even in the short run, officers were often pessimistic that their coaching would be followed. They still offered advice, but did not expect to see even small changes that might enhance the quality of animals' lives. "You always try to better the situation if you're there, although you find in most instances that it goes in one ear and out the other," warned one officer. Compared to their animal-inclined coworkers, police-oriented officers were more pessimistic about changing such behavior. For instance, one complaint involved a dog without adequate food, water, and shelter. Although the complaint was unfounded, the officer noticed that the respondent's dog needed to be neutered. He counseled the respondent as to why it was important to do this, where he could get it done, and how to get financial support. Nevertheless, he felt very pessimistic when leaving that the respondent would do anything, "We all come with a big mission. Then you face reality. It is a job. You can make a difference in certain cases, but that guy we saw this morning is not going to neuter his dog. I would almost bet on that, and there's nothing I can do. I have to let go of that because if I go home and think about it, I'll drive myself crazy."

Officers' pessimism was not unfounded. Some respondents rejected their advice and became angry because they thought of themselves as "humane." Advice was an insult or affront to them. As an illustration, an officer pointed to respondents who did not realize that doghouses could be very uncomfortable in hot weather. He described how respondents reacted when told to keep their pets under a tree instead of in a doghouse during the hottest days of summer. "Some people go nuts when you tell them this. It's more beneficial for the animal to be tied out underneath the tree than to be tied to the doghouse where it's not going to use the doghouse this time of year. If the dog was tied to a doghouse this time of year and was to use the doghouse, the doghouse would be like an oven. It's just not going to use it. I would prefer to see the dog sitting out in the rain than to be tied to a doghouse in the direct sun for eight hours a day."

Officers also expected respondents to reject their advice, especially when it exceeded the minimum required by law. Not being able to expect more left an ever present disparity between their own regard for animals and what they expected of respondents. As one officer said, "There's a lot of situations that we walk away from and I don't like it, but they [respondents] are doing the minimum that they have to by law. I've sort of tried to tell them things that they could do to make it better. But they could choose to or choose not to, and I can't do anything about it, so you just close it." Another officer talked about this disparity when it came to the psychological well-being of dogs: "The psychological needs of dogs are not met, never could be, and everyone's standard is going to be different. I don't go to a place and expect them to . . . I mean, my dog has been fed and is on the couch, spoiled rotten. I don't expect everyone to do that, but I also don't expect them to keep them chained twenty-four hours a day and never spend time with them. You try and tell them, but everyone's standards are going to be different."

In fact, most did not trust respondents even if they claimed to cooperate. One officer, only on the job for two months, confided, "I don't believe a word they say to me. I don't believe them when they tell me they are going to do something." They realized that their advice could be ignored by respondents and, if this happened, that little could be done. As one officer noted, "That's one of the difficulties of

Officers found it hard to believe that the owner of this neglected horse would quickly clean up its unsanitary stable and improve its care.

this job. You can educate, or try and educate, people as to the proper way to do things, but if the person looks at you and says, 'Screw you people, I'm going to do things the way I want to do them,' and if it's not a violation of the law, then you have to walk away." Another officer, for example, spoke to a respondent about the need to have his dog neutered. Although the respondent agreed to do this, the officer left the respondent's home believing that he would not do this. According to the officer, "It sounds like that guy's going to get his dog neutered, but no, I think he's not. Just the way he was acting, saying 'I'm not neutered, so why should my dog be?' You just know he's probably not going to do it. Deep down inside you'd like to take a person like that and bring him into the shelter where they have to euthanize so many animals and say, 'You do it,' but you can't."

As officers acquired more experience, their cynicism grew. They began to see telltale predictions of noncompliance in respondents' behaviors and lifestyles. For one, if they neglected their children or themselves, officers foresaw an inability or unwillingness to change. "You look at the way the person lives, and how much can we expect out of that person?" remarked one officer. Another observed, "If you go out and the dog looks okay, you can't say, 'Oh, you've gotta feed him dog food.' 'What dog food?' There's a lot of people who can't afford dog food, so they give them what they're eating. You go out there and see this bowl of mash, or whatever the heck it is, and you realize that was their dinner and that's what the dog gets." And yet another officer elaborated, "Sometimes it's kind of hard to sit there and explain to people that they should be caring for their animals in a certain way when they don't care for themselves as good or any better than they do their animals. Or they don't care for their kids any better. And yet you're telling them, 'You need to have all these stupid things for your animal,' but yet they don't have it for themselves or their kids." He went on to explain that this was not to excuse such respondents because they did not have to have their animals, "but the thing is, that you also have to look at the whole picture, too. So if someone is living in squalor, you can't expect them to give the dog steak. If you look at their house and their house is basically a shack that's falling down and their animals basically have a shack that's falling down, well, you know, everything's relative there."

Cynicism even colored their views of respondents who followed advice. Officers did not trust their motivations, believing that they only complied to avoid legal repercussions rather than to help animals. As one officer said, "We do mostly education. But the reason most people comply isn't because they want to do better for the animal. Most people comply, not all of them, but the majority comply because if they don't, they will be subject to court action." Indeed, officers argued that the threat of going to court was one of the few ways to motivate respondents. One officer noted, "Whenever I am working on something I say, 'Look, if you don't straighten this out, there is a possibility I may have to sign a complaint against you.' Try to tell them, 'I don't want to sign a complaint because it is paperwork for me, and once I sign a complaint, we have to go through with it. So do yourself a favor and correct it.' So you try to get them to think you are the good guy, you are trying to help them."

The "Knack"

Respondents often ignored simple and direct advice, especially when they were not violating the law. As one officer put it, "You try to get them to voluntarily comply with what you're trying to get them to do . . . in some cases, it takes a knack to do that." Part of the knack was for officers to present themselves as having more power than they actually had. Some of their power was illusory because it depended on mistaken assumptions made by respondents about what officers could do because they were like regular police. For instance, their mere appearance as law enforcement officers won some cooperation. Several officers commented that the dress and gear of police gave them extra "power" when dealing with people; as one said, "I have a certain amount of power. I have my presence. I have a gun belt, wear a gun, wear a holster, wear an OC [Oleoresin capsicum spray, also known as "pepper spray"], I carry extra ammunition, I carry handcuffs, the radio, the baton. All of those things present a certain picture and a certain message for people. If I showed up at someone's house and I didn't have a gun or I looked like the rag man, my boots weren't shining, it would be an uphill battle." He continued, "You want to go there and be able to say to them, 'I'm telling you, this is what you've got to do.' And hopefully, just from your presence, they're going to listen to you." Officers deliberately emphasized their presumed authority to get cooperation. To build on this illusory power, they sometimes let respondents know that their mistreatment of animals could be construed as a violation of law. For example, in one "no-shelter" case, two dogs were found in a yard, having only the area underneath a porch for shelter. The investigating officer felt that he could not, at the time, push the shelter issue because it was summer, although he was not sure if both dogs could fit under the porch at once to protect them from rain. Since no one was home, he left his card to be called back so he could "touch base" with the respondents and "warn them of the law." He speculated that just letting them know about the cruelty code might prompt them to provide better shelter for their dogs.

Some admitted that they carefully worded their statements to respondents so they could gain access to their property and animals. How they spoke to respondents made it possible to "go in giving people the attitude 'I have the right to look at these animals.' People are under a misconception. If people knew what you can do and what you couldn't do, we wouldn't get our job accomplished. You bullshit your way into a lot of situations." One officer used the following approach with a respondent. "I said to him, 'I'm going to go down and check on the dog.' He didn't say I couldn't go down and check on the dog. Until he tells me I can't go in his backyard and check on the dog, he's given me permission to go back and check on the dog. Just like I'll say to people, 'Why don't we take a look at the dog?' or 'I'm going to take a look at the dog and I'll come back and talk to you.'" Another officer took a different approach. "Sometimes I'll ask them if we can look at the dog. Or I'll say to them, 'Can we look at the dog?' I'm saying to them, 'I'm going to look at the dog.'" And another officer simply knocked on the respondent's door and said, "'I had a complaint. You've got some cats in poor condition. Where are the cats? I'd like to see them.' They invite you in and you look at the cats. All they have to tell you is, 'Screw you, get off my property. I don't have to talk to you.' And there's nothing you can do."

Aware that strictly interpreting the law could discourage responsible animal ownership, officers sometimes provided deliberately vague advice to respondents. They could create the impression that advice was legally required by "planting the seed," as one officer explained. "By law, you don't have to have water out for a dog all day, but I suggest that to people. Nobody ever questions you when you tell them the dog has to have water. I say, 'Gee, it's a hot day, put some water out for the dog.' But you can't say to them, 'Look lady, the law says you don't have to have water out,' because if you do you're kind of defeating your whole purpose of being there."

Part of the knack was to "control" interaction with respondents, knowing when feelings should be hidden from them. One officer talked about how he tried to control his anger, sometimes trying not to appear "pissed," while, at other times, using his anger constructively. "I try not to project an attitude where they see that I'm pissed off at them because if they can see I'm pissed off it has a couple of effects. Number one, they start to use that against you and you get more pissed off. On the other hand, I don't allow people to walk all over me either. I've sat there and said to people, 'Will you keep your mouth shut for a second so that I can tell you what I want to tell you?' Because you get to the point where, if you allow people to walk all over you, then you lose total control over the situation." Another officer talked about the importance of not appearing to be "pushy." He explained, "It depends on the individual. Sometimes you don't want to come across as too pushy because that has a detrimental effect. Like with the respondent we just visited. I tried to talk to him in a very reasonable and understanding way to see if I can get him to comply. I did let him know what the allegations were and kind of indirectly told him, without saying, 'The law says that you'll do this, this, and this.' It wasn't appropriate to be pushy with this person, based on what I had for information and based on the observations made."

Not being too pushy with respondents meant that officers had to work with complainants to resolve situations. For instance, in one case an officer tried to reduce tension between two neighbors that resulted from the complainant's dog running through the respondent's yard. The complainant alleged that the respondent tried to poison her dog, spray mace on it, and hit it with a broom. The officer asked the complainant to become a more responsible pet owner and to respect the respondent's wish for privacy. "Like I told the owner of the dog, 'You know this woman doesn't want the dog on her lawn.' He said, 'There is no leash law.' I said, 'That's besides the point. She wants her privacy. She doesn't want the dog in her yard. Keep it home. Tie it if you have to, but you shouldn't allow it to go over there. I mean, she's [respondent] wrong in doing what she's doing, and I'm going to let her know that, but you've got to kind of help out. I'm going to tell her that she can shoo him away and suggest to her that she take a hose out and spray him with a hose.'"

Sometimes controlling interaction called for more aggressive tactics. Stronger approaches were used to deal with "difficult" respondents who did not "work" with officers to correct problems. One officer, for instance, said that he employed an "in your face" strategy with respondents "who dictate to me how the call is going to go." Another officer claimed that he "accordingly modified" his "attitude" if respondents were not cooperative. Those taking this confrontational approach asserted authority to impress on difficult respondents their wrongdoing. One officer explained that he used his authority to one-up a respondent so as "not to be taken." As he said, "When someone takes a swing at you, you have to maintain one level above that so you don't get taken. Dealing with a respondent, I use the same philosophy. So if I knock on the door and I say 'Hi, I'm with the

MSPCA and we got a call on your dog.' And they go, 'What's your fucking problem pal? It's my fucking dog. I'll do what I fucking want.' I'm going to be more
like, 'Hey, I'm here to protect your dog, and you can't do what you want because
the law says you can't.'"

Asserting authority needed to be done carefully, otherwise presentations
crumbled. Respondents tuned into these presentations and were quick to discount officers. Even small details, if questionable or inconsistent, were read by
respondents as signs of weakness indicating that officers had less power than suggested. They could not be careless with their advice. First of all, they had to know
what they were talking about to respondents, since the latter could have substan-
tial veterinary knowledge about their animals. Officers lost credibility if they "pre-
tended" to know more than they did. Speaking about the importance of not pre-
tending, an officer said:

> You have to know what the hell you're talking about. I don't pretend
> to be an authority on things that I'm not an authority on. You get
> yourself in a lot of problems if you start to pretend to know things that
> you don't know because what ends up happening is people are able to
> read into it that this person is a phony. A lot of rookies will tend to
> buffalo their way through the thing, rather than just say, "I don't
> know, but I'll find out and I'll get back to you." Some respondents will
> try to pull something over on you. They may bullshit you all the way
> down the line. At that point they're saying, "What a friggin' phony this
> person is. He doesn't even know what the hell he's talking about. He's
> going to sit there and pretend he knows something that he doesn't
> know." And you lose your credibility.

Secondly, officers lost credibility if they failed to "back up" their words, as one
explained. He used the example of visiting a respondent's home in the middle of
winter for a "dog out without shelter" complaint. After telling the respondent that
he must get a doghouse, the response was "by when?" "They're trying to get you to
say, 'You have to have a doghouse by . . . say today's December 5, by December 8.'"
Of course, officers sometimes specified exact dates in very critical situations; for
example, the owner of a dog in need of urgent medical attention was told to take
it to a veterinarian the next day. However, if exact dates were given, "you better
back up what you're saying to them and do whatever the 'or else' is because if you

don't, you lose your credibility. After a while, people get the opinion that you're a bullshitter—that you don't back up what you are going to say. So a lot of times, I'll say, 'I'll be checking back.' 'When do you think you'll be checking back?' 'Well, I really don't know at this point, but I'll check back when I feel it's reasonable for you to have done what you should be doing.'"

Regardless of how officers presented themselves, respondents sometimes still ignored their advice. And if they could not be prosecuted, officers could do little. As one noted, "If it's not a violation, I really have no right to go back. Some people, you'll approach them. The animal will be in a situation that's not the best for them, but it's not the worst. You can try to improve it. Talk to them. But if they're like, 'Get the hell off my property you little . . .' or 'Don't ever come back here,' there's nothing you can do if they're not breaking the law." Another officer described a case where a dog did not have water: "Bottom line is, if they say, 'Screw you, I'm not going to leave water out there for the dog,' and the dog's condition doesn't reflect the fact that it's not being provided with adequate water, then at that point, yeah, you can educate them. But as far as prosecuting them, there is no prosecution as far as that's concerned." At these times, officers could only be clear and firm with their advice and warn of rechecks. Managing an obstreperous respondent, an officer illustrated this situation. The complaint involved a dog infested with fleas, suffering from a tumor, troubled with an ear infection, and allowed to run loose through the neighborhood. When the officer told the owner why he was visiting her, the respondent said that the dog was "not around anymore" and she had not seen it for two days. When asked about its tumor, the respondent admitted that it had a growth on its side. When asked about the fleas, the response was "I didn't really notice." Continuing, the officer said to her, "As soon as the dog comes back, I want you to make sure you notice. If the dog has those problems, you've got to get it to a vet or else you've got to take it to an animal shelter and get rid of the dog." She said, "I can't afford a vet," to which the officer replied, "When you decide what you're going to do, here's my card. But if I don't hear back from you, I'm going to be coming back."

If going to court was an option, this "next step" might be threatened when acceptable changes were not made. An officer described this graduated approach to working with respondents: "You start as reasonable and see if that works. See if by educating the individual that has an impact. If that doesn't work, then at that point you go to the next step." In one "no shelter, no water" complaint that continued over time, the officer visited a respondent for the second time because calls continued to come into the department about this animal's poor treatment. The respondent insisted that he left the dog outside for only a limited period, despite complaints saying it was outside all the time, regardless of weather conditions. The officer said, "Look, I've spoken to an individual and she says that yesterday it was ninety degrees and your dog was out from ten to two. I can't sit here for twenty-four hours a day. The only thing I can tell you is that one of your neighbors wants to get involved and will give me a statement that keeps track of the amount of days the dog is out. If she wants to keep track of these things and the weather conditions, and I feel it's adequate to pursue a court case, you're going to find that you're receiving a notice from the court." At that point, the officer has gone one step further. And in many cases, taking the next step forced compliance, albeit without good will on the respondent's part. When an officer investigated one case, he found a Lhasa Apso to be very matted, thin and underfed, with cataracts. "This dog was in real pitiful shape." He talked to the owner who started to cry when the discussion turned to humanely euthanizing his dog. He said, "I realize that, but I haven't had the heart to do it." The officer sat with the respondent and tried to reason with him, explaining that euthanasia was the right thing to do for this animal. When the officer returned two weeks later to see if the respondent took action, he found the dog still alive but looking "much worse." "And the guy's like, 'I'm at the point now, I really can't face the decision.'" The officer said to him, "I hate to put it to you this way, but you're just not being fair to the dog, and right now, the way you're keeping the dog, you're in violation of the law. I would really hate to have to take you to court, but if you don't do something fairly quickly, like within the next week or so, I'm going to end up having to pursue a court case against you." Two days later the respondent euthanized the dog. "Then he turns around and basically his attitude is, 'You're an asshole for making me put my dog to sleep.' He said basically, 'Yeah, I took the dog to the Animal Rescue League. Thanks for making me kill my dog.' That's okay, too. If it's easier for him to take out his madness or anger on someone else or blame someone else for having to have the dog put to sleep, I don't have a problem with that."

Court also might be threatened when respondents behaved like "jerks," similar to "assholes" who threaten the supervisory status of regular police (Van Maanan 1978). In fact, one officer devised a special coding system to indicate on his day sheets which respondents were particularly difficult by noting "AH," for asshole, next to a person's name. Some jerks lied or concealed information. An officer illustrated how he would use threats of court with a respondent who was suspected of but denied killing and disposing of his dog: "You tell the jerk 'If we find out different, if the animal was inhumanely killed, there is a good chance you could be prosecuted. So if the dog is here some place where we could check it, put it to bed, then it would behoove you now to come forward.' " Other jerks had

histories of evading officers. In one complaint of a kitten with a broken leg for sale in a pet store, the respondent had a long track record of complaints against him that he ignored. "If the injured kitten hasn't been treated and he doesn't do something right away with it, with a veterinarian, then I would take out complaints against this guy [store owner] in criminal court for cruelty because he's such a jerk. Since the day he opened his store . . . we went to the place once and we saw him hiding under the counter." When the officer investigated this case, he also found other violations beyond the original complaint, including wooden floors that could not be sterilized, aquaria that lacked surfaces for turtles to use, the absence of isola-

An officer inspects conditions in a pet store. Unsanitary conditions and/or inadequate space are not uncommon problems.

tion rooms, excessive feces in dog cages, and inadequate purchasing records. In his words, "I saw these same violations three times last summer. The thing was a mess. If we go there tomorrow, it will be the same thing. It's been a dump since the day he opened and nothing's been done." Finally, jerks were indifferent to the suffering of animals. One such respondent with a "bad attitude" was involved in a "dog without shelter or water" complaint. When his nineteen-year-old son answered the door, the officer explained to the young man that the extreme heat of July was very bad for dogs without water. Asking to see the dog in question, the officer was taken to a small shed under the back porch, where he saw several five-week-old puppies. The officer commented on how he could feel the heat coming out of the shed. He said, "No good. Why are they separated from the mother? They still need their mother." The young man replied, "My father said she's a bad mother because she won't nurse." At that moment the puppies headed toward the mother and started nursing. The officer repeated the specifics of the complaint, but the man seemed evasive and unwilling to provide water and adequate shelter, blaming it on his father's wishes. The officer made him take all the dogs downstairs into the cooler basement and handed him his card, saying, "If your father doesn't want to go to court have him call me." Driving away from the property, the officer confided, "I mean, this kid was really giving me an attitude. And he didn't even care that the dog didn't have any water and it's ninety something degrees out."

Threats of court action were useful. If nothing else, they gave respondents "something to think about." As one officer noted, "We try to educate them and at the same time to warn them that 'You did this. It was a mistake. It wasn't severe enough for me to take you to court at this point, but if it happens again then a complaint will be issued against you.' And that gives them something to think about." Threats to "sign a complaint" could be made to gain respondents' compliance, as an officer explained. "You've just gotta work with these people until it [officer's advice] gets done. And then you tell them, 'I've been trying to work with you, and you have just been stringing me along. I've had it. I am going to sign a complaint against you.' Now they scurry. Most the time, they will scurry and get things done." Officers acknowledged that warnings sometimes failed, but they created a chilling effect where respondents knew they were being watched. "I'll warn them. But a lot of people know they shouldn't kill, and they do it anyway. So it's sort of, what good is a warning going to do? But in some cases, it's sort of to let some people know that they are being watched and that just might stop them from doing something," said one officer. And some threats worked because respondents might want to avoid the time and expense of going to court. This was especially true for horse owners and farmers, claimed one officer. "I think mostly with them, if you tell them what the law is and they know the law, then they have to make a decision that 'I'm either going to do it or I'm going to have to go to court and explain why I didn't do it.' And most of them don't want to take the time to come to court, so they just do it."

However, threats could be made carelessly and backfire. For instance, some respondents "shut down" when court was mentioned, blocking what officers said or being unreceptive to them in the future. As one staff member warned, "If you use 'SPCA' and you threaten them that if they don't do something, you're going to take them to court, you're probably not going to get through to the person and you're just going to create problems. Next time, they won't let you in." They also exercised caution not to threaten court if winning seemed very unlikely. This assessment influenced how much pressure to put on respondents during investigations. An officer gave the following example: "Sure, I could have said, 'That's a violation of the law relating to the dogs in the sun and blah, blah, blah.' She could have really went off. If I back myself in a corner like that, she could tell me to go stuff it. Then if I really felt that strong about the violation of law, I'd have to go to court, and I'd probably be laughed out of court." Given the precarious status of officers as law enforcers, their authority could be further impaired if court action were threatened but not carried out. They needed to follow through when reaching this point. According to one officer, "You never want to tell them that you are going to take them to court unless you are going to take them because if you say that, and you don't take them, your credibility is gone." Officers, then, were careful not to threaten court action unless they meant it. Damage to their presentation of professional self would be irreparable. For instance, one officer described what he did after leaving his business card for a respondent who did not telephone him:

> I leave a card for people not home. After a few days, depending on how serious the allegations are, I go back and I leave another card. In some cases, leave a third card for the people. And usually when I leave a third card, I'll write, "I've left two previous cards, no response, law attached." And that gets marked down as a warning, if I know that the allegations are somewhat legitimate. If I know that the allegations are such that I might want to pursue it further, I might in some cases put on the card, "Failure to contact me may result in court action without further notice." Most of the time, if you put that on the card, the next day the people are on the friggin' horn. But I don't do that unless I know that there's at least—and I don't put "will result," I put "may result"—I never do that unless I know that there's a possibility that I might be pursing some type of further action. You never draw lines in the sand unless you're willing to step over the line, the reason being you lose your credibility. If I was to put on something, "Failure to contact me will result in court action" and two or three weeks down the pike or a month down the pike the people don't get a notice to appear in court and then six months from then I get another complaint on this individual, and you go out there and you have to catch them there, and the first thing out of their mouth is gonna be, "I thought you were going to take me to court three months ago."

Clearly, there was a limit to how many times respondents could be warned before animal police lost all credibility.

In some cases, definitive court action had to be pursued, as one officer noted: "I spoke to John Smith a couple of times, and I finally got to the point . . . I'm not going to keep going out and speaking to someone if I feel there's a problem there. You get to the point where I'll speak to them a couple of times, but how many times are you going to speak to him? After a while they know you're just bullshitting them, that you're not going to do anything, and it loses its effect after a while. You can only speak to someone so many times." Officers felt that these respondents only complied if court action were taken. For example, one respondent repeatedly ignored an officer's advice to build an appropriate shelter for his farm animals. Upon failing to do so, the officer filed a complaint, which appeared to push the respondent's behavior in the right direction for the no-shelter violation as well as for his continuing neglect of the animals. The officer recounted the case:

I'd been working with him all summer the same way—shelter, shelter, shelter. "Yeah, okay, I'll take care of it, I'll take care of it." Well come the late fall, thank God the weather has been good, the shelter is still not up. Then he tells me, "I'll have it done by next week." I said, "John, you have until next week. If it's not up by next week, I'm signing the complaint." So I go back the next week. No shelter. So I went down and I signed the complaint. Two days later he calls me, "The shelter is all done." I said, "It's too late. I signed the complaint." So we went into court. He comes in and told the clerk that he put up the shelter, but I was concerned because he had a couple of sheep that were lame. A lot of your hoofed animals get infections up in the crack, they call it hoof rot. You've got to take care of it. I told this guy that. He said, "I'll get the vet down." I said, "You don't have to get a vet as long as you take care of it," and I told him how to do it and I told him to put lime down in the area to keep infection out. He didn't do it. So when I went back, the shelter was fine, excellent as a matter of fact. But there were still two sheep that were still on the uneven side. They still weren't walking properly. So I told the clerk that I was satisfied with the shelter now, but there were still two sheep that were lame. So he said, "I'm going to give you two weeks to correct it or get a vet in there. You go back and recheck and if everything is okay, I'm going to dismiss it." So I went back yesterday. Everything is fine. The sheep are fine, so you withdraw the complaint.

After this encounter, the officer warned the respondent that any future mistreatment of animals would result in immediate legal action. As he said, "Hopefully now he is going to know that if I go there and see a problem, I'm not . . . I told him, 'I'm not even going to fool around with you. I'm not even going to call you up. I'm just going to go down to court and sign a complaint and this time it's going to stay there.' And the clerk told him the same thing."

Other strategies beside threatening court pushed respondents to comply. An effective one was to suggest that their animals would be seized. These threats were veiled when officers did not intend to get a court order to take animals. In one case, an officer investigating a no-shelter complaint in a multi-family dwelling spoke to families in three different units of the building, but no one admitted to owning the dog. The officer left his card and said he would give the owner a week to call him, especially since weather conditions were not bad and the dog would be safe and comfortable outside. However, if the owner failed to do this, he said, "I'll go back with a Boston police officer. If they said, 'I don't own it,' I would have said, 'No one owns the dog, okay.' I would have taken the dog, put him in the back of my car. Anyone calls and says that's my dog, I would have said, 'I was at the first floor—not my dog—second floor—not my dog—third floor—not my dog. If it's nobody's dog, it's my dog.' When you take an animal, the calls come real quick." In another case, an officer made a veiled threat by suggesting to the respondent, but never actually saying, that without proper veterinary care her dog would have to be euthanized, and if she refused euthanasia, humane law enforcement would get it done. The case involved a second complaint of a dog chewing its infected bloody leg. After visiting the respondent's veterinarian, the officer was told that if the dog's leg did not get treated, it would face amputation. When he visited the respondent, the dog appeared to have an active leg infection, excreting pus and causing the dog to limp. He told the respondent that the dog needed veterinary treatment to save its leg, and that this might involve amputation. The respondent, however, said that she could not afford the forty dollars needed to pay the veterinarian. Although the officer told her about discounts for needy clients, the respondent was indifferent to these suggestions. The officer then said that if treatment were not sought, the dog might have "to be put to sleep." The respondent seemed confused and asked what that meant. The officer replied, "Put down . . . euthanized," at which point the respondent understood the officer and began to cry, as she stroked her dog. The officer asked to be called the next day and told what she was going to do.

Forcing the surrender of animals, whether signed over by respondents or the result of court order, was another option, but one officers had mixed feelings about using. For example, threatening to take animals could backfire. As an example, one officer pointed to a rookie's mistake because her aggressiveness jeopardized future interactions with the respondent. He noted, "Officer Kathy went out to one of these cat collectors, and she was real tough, and she ended up getting them signed over. The lady still has about sixteen cats. She ended up hiring a vet to come in and take care of the cats. And now, I can guarantee that Officer Kathy is not going to get back into that house. I went the other way. I bent over backwards for one of these animal collectors." Taking animals also

This cat was seized by officers and sent to a shelter, where it still faces an uncertain future.

could cause significant emotional distress for respondents and their families. Speaking about this problem, an officer gave the example of "needy" families whose deprived situation might call for surrendering animals. Doing this, however, could seriously disturb children, if present. He elaborated, "You have cases where it's a family that's having a hard time and can't afford the feed or the dog or cat needs medical attention. It's real hard when you go in and you got some children there, and they're not even taking care of the kid properly. They're living in a dump or whatever and you have this dog and because they can't really afford to take care of it, do you take it away from them and upset the children like that?" Nor were children the only ones upset by surrenders. Adult respondents, too, could be very distressed by this. An officer described one such case that surprised him because he assumed that the respondent was a "cruel person" until he started crying:

I had a case where I went out and there was a Rottweiler, and the dog's leg was broken and it eventually fell off the dog. It was up by the elbow, and it was just the bone sticking out. It upset me very much. I was real hard on the party and said, "You'd better sign this over to me, and if you don't I'm going to lock you up right now." And so they agreed and I called for the ambulance to come out. The ambulance came out and the guy turned around when we put the dog in the ambulance and he was crying. He had a love for the dog. The dog loved him. You must get a sense whether the respondents are caring for the animal or whether they don't give a damn. Like this guy with the Rottie sounds like he cared for the dog but just didn't have money. I turned around and read it all wrong. When I got there, in my mind he was just a cruel person. And it made me think when I saw his emotions.

Forcing surrender could trouble officers too, making them reluctant to use this strategy because they knew that animals might be killed as a result. One spoke about this conflict: "You end up turning them over to the shelter, but they end up being euthanized because when you take them away, these animals need special care, medical attention, and you just don't have the money to do it. So you're kind of signing a death warrant for the animal. So then you have to turn around and decide, is it better to have a minimum life and be alive or is it better to be dead?" Although officers rationalized surrendering by saying that some animals were better off being killed than staying with cruel or neglectful people, they still found these situations to be profoundly sad and unfortunate. For all these reasons, officers loathed pushing for surrender except in the most extreme and irresolvable cases.

Indeed, these tactics suggest that, despite good intentions and skillful casework, officers' pursuit of compliance could have undesirable consequences. For one, they claimed that being investigated outraged some respondents, who displaced their anger by further assaulting their animals. At these times, officers felt they created more cruelty by doing their work. As one said of such situations, "I have a real hard time walking away from half the houses I go to because if it's something like beating a dog with a coat hanger, they might get mad at me when I leave and take it out on the dog." Just as some respondents took out their anger on animals, visits from humane officers could trigger abuse against humans. During one investigation, the officer "had to leave the dog there until I could find him [husband-respondent] because if I took the dog, I knew he was going to come back and beat the shit out of her [wife]." Also, investigating cases could ignite or intensify neighborhood feuds. "I've had people say, 'It's that son of a bitch next door,' and they actually stomp by you and go bang on their neighbor's door. And I'm just standing there, like, 'Please don't open the door, please, please.'" In one case, the respondent spoke angrily about the presumed neighbor-complainant, who she claimed had been giving her "a lot of trouble since moving in." The respondent insisted that now she was "going to make her [complainant] life like hell." Some officers claimed to have witnessed outbursts and even fights between neighbors, as happened in the following case: "One time a woman made a call and I'm there on the porch talking to the guy who she made the call to. She lived in the same house on the second floor and they started this big fight on the porch, like a verbal fight. I was like, 'Forget it.' The people were screaming at each other. I'm just standing there like, 'Okay, if somebody punches somebody or stabs somebody, I'm going to jump in and arrest somebody.'" Although unpleasant to encounter, these unanticipated negative consequences of investigation were infrequent, or at least officers rarely heard about them. For the most part, the knack enabled astute officers to foresee adverse outcomes, thereby sidestepping problems and effectively managing respondents.

◆ ◆ ◆

Officers dealt with many cases that barely qualified under the law as cruelty, and their authority to enforce them was precarious. They behaved more like humane educators than law enforcers when first trying to correct these problems. Education, though, often failed. When this happened, officers improvised and used the knack. This incremental approach to changing the behavior of respondents began with friendly suggestions and graduated to sterner warnings, until threats of court action were the only alternative left to produce the desired treatment of animals. These informal strategies nudged respondents toward behaving more humanely. These approaches did not always work, but they were all that officers had. Noncompliance, regardless of the strategy used, was expected more often than not.

Apart from their unreliability as tools to change behavior, using education or the knack posed certain risks to officers. As they adopted increasingly more threatening or aggressive approaches with difficult respondents, they tried to preserve their image as law enforcement professionals. Doubting respondents easily challenged this feigned authority. When this happened, it threatened officers' self-worth. Like regular police officers (Meehan 1992), loss of face (Goffman 1967) could lead to loss of authority, forcing them to counteract these incidents with more face work to sustain the appearance of authority. Knowing that they had very little real power at their disposal if challenged, such face work made officers uneasy. They walked on sociological thin ice.

Resorting to these strategies had a sociological price. While they were necessary adaptations to work with respondents, these techniques subverted officers' role as law enforcers. The very actions they took to instill humane care reproduced society's larger ambivalence about the nature and importance of animals, an ambivalence that is just as likely to treat animals as objects or tools as it is to see them as valued companions (Arluke and Sanders 1996). Facing this conflict, officers could not exert more authority because they had so little legitimacy to do so, given their focus on animal cruelty. With mixed public support for their efforts, they found it difficult to play the police side of their roles as humane law enforcers. Instead, officers did the best they could to assist needy animals by educating respondents or using the knack with them, but doing so degraded their own image. It chipped away at what little authority they had, furthering the public's confusion over humane law enforcement and, indirectly, the importance of combating cruelty.

In this cultural and professional context, officers occasionally prosecuted cases when the knack failed or when cruelty was most deplorable. The response of courtroom officials to prosecuting cruelty, like officers' experience investigating cases, also reflected our society's ambivalence toward animals and confusion about the importance of humane law enforcement. As we see in the next chapter, officers struggled to adapt to the often disappointing and frustrating reality of court. They did so with flexibility and resiliency, despite facing many judicial challenges.

5

It's Just a Dog

> A perfect case is where the dog gets seen to, the person
> gets locked up, and you go to court and the judge is not
> sympathetic, but he's open-minded enough where he
> doesn't say, "Officer, it's just a dog." I've had a judge say
> that to me. "It's just a dog." . . . The worst part is the in-
> different judge.

As law enforcers, humane officers knew that the ultimate standard for evaluating
their work would be how they fared in court. Certainly, from the novice's view as
well as the laity's, the standard for judicial success was to win guilty verdicts and
stiff punishments that fit the severity of crimes. However, officers quickly realized
that it was difficult to negotiate the court system or win just solutions. On the
contrary, rookies encountered a judicial system that seemed indifferent to, if not
dismissive of, cruelty to animals. One exasperated officer underscored this sentiment: "I get up in the morning. I put my uniform on. I go out and whatever I do,
I feel like I'm just spitting into the wind because of what the court system does to
me. I have this thing that if I did my job perfectly, and if the laws were perfect, and
I could enforce the laws perfectly, people would actually listen to me and I could
get people to care about their animals. But I can't make somebody care about that
dog." To rookie and experienced officers alike, court officials impeded their efforts to reduce the suffering of animals.

This frustration was shared with regular police around the world. They too believe that court officials disempowered them, leading to extensive cynicism in the ranks (e.g., Rigakos 1995). It would be easy to imagine similar cynicism among humane officers, given the response of courts to animal cruelty cases. However, as we see, humane officers developed and maintained a view of themselves as effective law enforcers by redefining what constituted a success in court and by looking for other kinds of successes out of court.

Experiencing Court

Officers believed that courtroom officials diminished the seriousness of cruelty by not hearing complaints, dismissing cases, rendering not guilty verdicts, or imposing extremely weak punishments. This courtroom reality disappointed rookies because they hoped to win guilty verdicts and stiff sentences. Rare were moments like the following: "This is what happened. I got enough probable cause on John Smith to get a warrant. We went in and we seized his dogs. He had dogs in airline crates, steel crates, and they were that deep in feces. There was one wire-hair fox terrier that had a ball of manure underneath its neck the size of a softball. I charged him with a couple of things. We were successful in court. He was found guilty."

More typically, they felt "worn down" by the many respondents who violated regulations, but never ended up in court or, if they did, received little if any punishment. One rookie gave the following example: "Like we'll go in and do pet store inspections and do the same inspection all the time, and they're always flunking, but nothing's ever done." Many officers remembered their rookie frustration and anger over cases that merited guilty verdicts, only to be found not guilty or dismissed by judges. As one newcomer said, "I'm never going to be satisfied with the verdicts just because most animal things are continued without a finding [cases dropped if respondents avoid arrest for a period of time determined by judges] or probation for six months." Another officer vividly recalled his first big legal disappointment. The case involved two horses that were starved to death. The judge found the respondent guilty, but his lawyer appealed the case. The jury heard the facts and two veterinarians testified that the horses died from malnutrition. "I just couldn't believe that the jury found him not guilty. I yelled, 'You gotta be kidding me.' It just came out. The judge banged the thing and said, 'Who is that yelling back there?' I told him I was the officer. He said, 'One more outburst like that and I'll have you in contempt of court.' I just couldn't believe it. I kept telling my boss, 'I can't believe this.' I busted my hump and a jury finds this man not guilty. So that was my first. I didn't believe it." Even more seasoned officers could be frustrated, especially when they tried to prosecute the same respondent many times with the same disappointing results. One officer described such a case, although he expected to take this respondent to court again. For ten years, he struggled with a farmer who kept his animals in unsanitary conditions without proper shelter. "This is the type of thing gets you frustrated fairly quick," he said. Although the officer took the respondent to court six times, outcomes were always disappointing. The last time he did so, the respondent's lawyer plea bargained the case. "They put him on pre-trial probation with me having inspection rights there which means, for all intents and purposes, he got nothing. I did want a guilty on him because I knew I'd be dealing with him time and time again."

When respondents were punished, it could be a mere "slap on the hand." Penalties for cruelty almost never seemed just and fitting, diminishing the significance of the crime from the officers' perspective. In one typical outcome, a woman was taken to court several times over one year for starving horses, getting only a "continued without a finding" judgment each time. The investigating officer told the respondent after the last starvation complaint, "I told you before, if you get into a situation, pick up the phone. We can find them homes, but you don't let the animal suffer." With the latest complaint, officers decided to take the respondent's horses and go to court. According to the testifying officer, "I got up and told the judge about why I thought she should be found guilty because there was another situation back in 1993 where the animals were just about starved to death, and we gave her a break. And now here we are doing the same thing over again. He didn't want to hear any part of it. Continued without a finding for one year and not have any horses for that amount of time. That's a slap on the hand. I'm sad, but did my job." Results such as these left even seasoned officers feeling uneasy about their lack of power and influence over the outcome of cruelty cases.

They had several explanations for their courtroom disappointment. For one, officers thought that officials dismissed them as law enforcers and therefore did not take their cases seriously. One recalled how a defense attorney referred to him in court. "I got pissed off, but what am I going to say in front of a judge? The defense attorney came up to the judge and said, 'The dog officer came up to his door and saw the dog.' I felt like saying, 'Gee, did somebody else come because

I'm a police officer?' It bothers me to some extent. I don't like being called a dog officer. We work hard and we have to go to the police academy, so we should get some recognition." Another officer also was disturbed by a similar comment, saying, "Like yesterday, I'm in court. And the DA is talking, and he goes, 'Your honor, the animal control worker, Tim Smith [the humane officer] has been there several times.' I wanted to yell out, 'I'm not with animal control!' You know what I mean? He didn't know."

Second, courtroom officials seemed to trivialize animal cruelty. For example, one officer felt uncomfortable pursuing a cruelty case in court because it involved a pigeon that a boy killed with a BB gun. He described what happened, "He [respondent] thought it was a joke, like we couldn't do anything. So I charged him. A neighbor saw it, came forward, was in court every time, even went out and got the pigeon for me as evidence. So I had an autopsy performed and it showed that the animal died as a result of being shot with a BB gun. But even the assistant district attorney in that case was kind of smirking about it. I did feel kind of embarrassed bringing in charges to a court on a pigeon, but then I said, 'Why should I? It's an animal.'" More

This case of pigeon darting was not taken seriously by court officials.

than "smirking," one officer recalled a case where a judge's joking about an animal's name took away from the seriousness of the case: "The judge made a joke of it. The cat's name was Fluffernutter. The district attorney wanted guilty, two years probation, and restitution. And when she [owner] told him the cat's name, he said 'Fluffernutter, isn't that something we put on sandwiches?' The court burst out. I could tell where this was going. The man was continued without a finding for one year." In another case, a woman allowed her five cats to stay outside; one was injured in a leg-hold trap set by an annoyed neighbor. After hearing the case, the judge made an offhand comment that hurt the case. According to the officer, "You get a judge like this one . . . he made a comment, 'Oh, I knew this woman who used to have a house full of cats. I wouldn't even go there.'"

Nor were attorneys and judges the only ones who disregarded animal cruelty cases. Clerks would too. One officer, for example, questioned their sympathy and competence. "They can be jerks and they aren't going to do anything for you anyway. You know, Westville court is a good example of it. The guy down there could care less about cruelty stuff or animal stuff, so don't bother. That's what he tells you." In one case of a dog that nearly died of heat exhaustion, allegedly caused by inappropriate kennel transportation, an officer claimed that the clerk said, "'Well, you know, the dog lived, didn't it? The dog didn't die, right?' So they didn't issue the complaint. Well, the dog shouldn't have been transported the way it was and it shouldn't have gotten to that point and the guy was definitely wrong, so that's one where it's like, 'It doesn't have to die for it to be . . .'" In gestures and remarks such as these, cruelty's significance seemed to be diminished. From the officers' perspective, this attitude partly explained their courtroom failures.

Third, to be taken seriously in court, cruelty had to be extreme, and even then it could be disregarded. As one officer said, only "drastic" cases had a chance. For example, a severely matted dog was not bad enough because of the absence of visible sores that would help the court see it as a victim of cruelty. According to a staff member, "It was like, 'Where's his butt? Where's his head?' And we got turned down for that complaint. Being that matted, you may not be able to say the dog was in pain, but there's going to be a certain amount of discomfort with the mats. It's gotta be heavy, weighing on him, and discomforting every time he moves. But something like that, why does there have to be sores? It shouldn't have to be so outrageous that it's dead. I think sometimes its gotta be that drastic for them to think it's cruelty. It's gotta be an actual beating or stabbing or death." If complaints were issued and cases went to court, officers felt that they, too, had to be extreme to have a chance of being taken seriously by judges. As one officer said, "Especially around here, with a dog with no shelter, unless it's really suffering, courts don't want to hear that." Another humane law enforcement agent compared the case of a badly beaten dog to that of a harassed cat. "I think if it was a beating or somebody really hurt the animal, they are a little more compassionate. But when it's something like 'Your honor, this man has a garden and these cats shouldn't be in the garden,' he's probably saying, 'Well, I have a garden, and if the cats were in it, I'd probably be a little ticked.' Unless you really have something that you know a court is going to say, 'This is disgusting, this is horrible,' nothing will happen." Similarly, another officer spoke of a judge who, despite his sympathy for the mistreatment of animals, only took seriously the most extreme cases of cruelty while ignoring others. As the officer said, "I've talked to the judge in charge of the district court. The really bad ones, he's great with. Someone's beating an animal, starving an animal, he'll send them to jail. But if the court feels that way, you're not going to get anywhere taking in violations of rules and regulations."

Even extreme cases could fail in court, leaving officers disappointed with the justice system. One talked about losing such a case and how it made her feel. It involved a young girl who said that her twelve-year-old indoor, declawed cat got outside and was lost. After a month without finding the cat, her neighbor told her that his tenant killed the cat. He overheard the tenant say, "I killed a cat the other day. If I see any more cats I'm going to kill them. I'm sick of them going to the bathroom all over the place." From the tenant's description, the landlord assumed that the murdered cat was the complainant's animal and told her so. He also gave a statement that the respondent hated cats. She responded by confronting the alleged killer, who slammed the door in her face. She then called the police, who investigated the case. The respondent said he did kill the cat. His first explanation for killing it, according to the officer, was that "It jumped at him, and it scared him, so he went and grabbed a hockey stick and hit it in the head and it died." His story changed somewhat over time. Later, he said that there was a cat in the basement but he thought it left the house. He was carrying a hockey stick when the cat jumped out and startled him. So when the cat jumped at him, he threw his hands up and the hockey stick went flying in the air and accidentally hit the cat, killing it. The complainant and her mother came to court, as did the respondent and his wife. The troubled officer said, "The clerk said that the only thing he did wrong was having failed to report having killed a cat. I was totally dysfunctional. I'm just starting to get my gusto back. I put a lot into it. A lot of emotional time."

Fourth, officers felt that if court officials perceived respondents as "doing" something for their animals, however modest, then a complaint would not be officially issued. In one case, an officer considered taking a respondent, who had failed to trim the hooves of his cows, to the hearing stage so that the state could issue a complaint. He decided against this, however, because the respondent called a veterinarian, making the officer's case weaker. In his words, "The thing is, he is doing it [trimming the hooves]. Once he starts doing it, if I were to go into court with him, he'll say, 'I had the vet in. I had the guy come down and trim the feet. And yes, they are hard to get a hold of.' So now the clerk is going to be like,

'Well, the guy's trying. What do you want?' So, once I go into court and he says, 'I've had the vet here,' they are not going to give you a hearing."

Finally, judges also appeared to be reluctant to render guilty verdicts or stiff sentences, contributing to their dismissive image. As one officer said, "With misdemeanor offenses, which cruelty to animals is, they [judges] don't want to give somebody a record. So they turn around and go without a finding for two years, and then it will be dismissed. What happens is, you could have the same person in two years later and because there's no record, you can't do anything about it." The court's dismissiveness, officers argued, was not only because cases involved animals per se, but because most criminal cases in general were rarely punished sternly by judges. As one officer said, "After you are on the job for a while, you realize that other crimes get the same thing. Even felony, B and E's, assault and batteries with dangerous weapons—those charges get reduced eventually and the people come out with continued without a finding. I think it's the system." So if judges heard cruelty cases, officers learned not to expect harsh penalties and, when this happened, it was because respondents committed other crimes taken more seriously in court. Commenting on this courtroom reality, an officer observed, "The judge isn't going to send anybody away for cruelty to animals because we're not sending away bank robbers, rapists, and all that. I've had one case where they were sent away for six months, but the reason was that the police department wanted this person and I had the proof, so the district attorney and everybody put on a lot of pressure to send him away. But in my mind, it wasn't because of the cruelty, it was other issues."

Officers not only expected to lose in court, for whatever reason; they questioned the value of winning, should it happen. One reason why officers felt futile was that abuse could rarely be stopped, short of removing animals from respondents' homes, and even this did not necessarily prevent respondents from getting more animals to abuse. Speaking of this problem, one officer described herself as a "cleaner" of "people's messes," but not someone who could prevent the abuse of animals. In her words, "Stuff is going to happen anyway. I can't stop things from happening. Maybe if that guy this morning gets a doghouse, I can stop the dog from freezing to death but I can't stop people from abusing their animals. So it's sort of, I'm more of a cleaner. You come in and clean up people's messes, and the mess unfortunately is an animal suffering. It's like, I didn't create this mess. I'm sorry that you're on welfare and can't afford to feed yourself, let alone your dog. But your dog doesn't know you're on welfare. It's sort of, 'I can't solve all your problems.'"

Another reason why it seemed futile was that abuse could continue for many months before being heard in court. As one veteran officer pointed out, "When you get into the court system, you're talking probably six months to a year to get the problem solved. You have the problem. What do you do with the animal for that length of time? And there's the possibility that you could put it back into shape if it was in poor condition, and the court turns around and gives it back to them." Indeed, returning abused animals to owners after going to court, or allowing them to have more, seemed to question the value of prosecuting anyone. An officer gave the example of a case involving alleged "starving of horses." The respondents were unwilling to turn over custody of the animals to humane law enforcement, so the investigating officer seized the animals and took the case to court. Much to the officer's chagrin, he noted, "What happened with the courts was there was no finding, basically for two years. And the court turned around and gave them five of the eleven horses back after we got them nice and fat, which is kind of crazy but it's beyond my control." Even if respondents were found guilty and fined, some officers felt this accomplished little. One staff member elaborated this view: "It doesn't make any difference half the time. They are still going to get another animal. It's going to happen again. They didn't learn anything from it. They just learned to take it indoors. Take the abuse indoors, out of the public's view, take it indoors, where they can't be seen." Some of their reluctance stemmed from frustration with the big picture. Officers doubted the value of winning verdicts, since such decisions did not undo harm done to animals. An officer provided an example of this dilemma: "My husband said to me, 'So did you win in court? How'd you do?' And it's like, I don't even answer him because it's like, the horse is dead, what difference does it make? We found one of the horses fell down into the hold and died. You can't prevent it. That's a horrible death. I mean the conditions of the probation were very good, but as far as I'm concerned, that horse is dead. So what good really came out of that?"

Since winning seemed of questionable value, on the rare occasions when it occurred, officers learned to see the prosecution of most cases as a waste of time and energy. Some were reluctant to take respondents to court because of the time and energy required to do so, unless cases were relatively serious and/or there had been continued problems with difficult respondents. As one officer said, "You don't drag everyone you meet into court. There's certainly a lot of things that go on out there than can use court action, but taking someone to court's a pain in the neck too. It takes a lot of time. You've got to go see the clerk. You've got to take some time to go to court. You go to court for the day, basically, you waste a day." Another departmental member compared rookies to more experienced officers in this regard: "There are definitely some [officers] that have been here for a while who feel that dragging people into court is not a big deal anymore. You know, with a newer officer, you want to get them into court. You want to prosecute. The other ones, they've been to court. Court can be a bigger pain in the ass than anything else and they just want the problem solved." Indeed, given the time and energy involved, plus the likelihood of losing, officers often felt they could accomplish more outside of court to improve an animal's situation. By looking at each complaint's "big picture," they asked themselves what they hoped to achieve with the respondent and whether going to court was necessary to achieve these aims. As one officer said, "I look at what I want out of this person, not what will the end result be. Like if a respondent is surrendering their animals and you know they're not going to get more, why prosecute them?"

Overall, officers had many reasons to be cynical about successfully prosecuting complaints. Given the court's dismissive attitude toward cruelty, they expected cases not to go forward or to be managed laxly if heard by judges and, if heard and found guilty, to wonder if such outcomes ultimately helped animals.

Feeling Effective

Officers learned to see their efforts as worthwhile and valuable, despite discouraging courtroom experiences. One tactic was to increase the likelihood of advancing and winning cases by only prosecuting those complaints having a reasonable chance of getting into court and being received favorably by judges. Other, weaker complaints were avoided because they were unlikely to make it to court, let alone result in guilty sentences. Officers anticipated that judges would see the latter as frivolous complaints.

One type of weak complaint involved "lower" animals, since officers realized that the abuse of "higher" animals would be taken more seriously by judges. Species closer to humans were more likely taken to court, even if lower animals were equally harmed. Discussing the decision not to prosecute a case involving five mice that were starved to death, the officer noted, "I think it would have been different if it were a dog. I think [the senior officer] would have allowed me to charge her [if she killed a dog] because a court's going to look at a mouse as 'Hit the road. It's not an animal. It's a mouse.' But I think everyone personalizes more with a dog."

Another type of weak case involved unreasonable complaints, such as those caused by bad timing. One officer investigated a complaint of a Husky without shelter or water, but assumed that the judge would not hear this case because of the pleasant late spring weather. In his words, "No shelter this time of the year really is a moot point. Sometimes we have a difficult time even in the winter getting shelter complaints through the court because of misconceptions courts have and judges have as far as what animals require or whatever. Summer time, I wouldn't even try and pursue a shelter case." Similarly, another officer felt that her hands were tied in a cruelty case because it was summer and only involved a "no-shelter" complaint. However, if the respondent ignored warnings and her dog died of exposure in the winter, going forward seemed more reasonable. "No court is going to look at this case. But if I went back in late September, and they still didn't have a doghouse, and I warned them again, and they still didn't get one, and it's December, and there's snow on the ground, and the dog froze to death and I get him into court, I can say, 'I warned them in July they needed a shelter. I warned them in September.' The court is more apt to issue the complaint because I gave them warnings and I checked back and I gave them a few opportunities to rectify the situation."

Certain characteristics of respondents also made for weak cases. For example, officers might not prosecute cases because of the respondent's advanced age. In one case of alleged unsanitary keeping of cats, the investigating officer said, "There wasn't enough food for the cats. It was unsanitary. I couldn't get through to her dealing with the cats, but what the heck am I going to do? There's no way a court . . . it was unsanitary, but a court would have said, 'You're picking on an elderly woman.' And I could just see the judge pointing his finger at me, telling me I was a bad girl for taking her to court." Other factors beside the respondent's age influenced the decision not to prosecute. If respondents appeared "remorseful," especially in cases not involving domestic animals, officers were less inclined to take court action. This happened with a woman who allegedly left four hamsters in her car on a very hot day, causing two of them to die from hyperthermia and dehydration and two others to be euthanized later. Although the investigating officer felt that the respondent should have been taken to court, he was overruled by more senior department members, who felt that certain factors argued against doing that. He noted: "They [senior department members] do not think that it would be a good idea to charge her because she's a mother of four kids and she didn't know any better and she sounded remorseful. But for something like that that's so blatant, I don't care how stupid you are. You still should pay for that because those animals died a painful death because of you." Another officer familiar with this case added, "It's real frustrating. I understand why [the senior officer] doesn't want to charge them in court. They'd probably say 'continued without a finding for six months' or something like that because the court would just basically dismiss it anyway if I took a mother of four to court, it was just an accident, she didn't know. And that would make me look bad—picking on the mother."

Once an appropriate case was selected, officers focused on the process of getting it into court. Like regular police officers, who focus on setting the criminal process into motion (Bittner 1990), the goal of animal police was to get cruelty in front of court officials. As one officer said, "My job is to bring a case to court, and if the courts don't find that there is enough there to go forward with, that's their decision. My job is to bring it forward so that they can make that determination." Seasoned officers could even be quite sure of failure but still go to court by not focusing on the trial or verdict as the outcome. As one explained: "Over the years, I have changed because you've been doing it for so long, you know more or less what's going to happen. You try not to think that way. You start to think negative, but you can't, you have to think positive. And whatever happens, happens. You have done your part. You have brought the facts forward. You have addressed the court. Now it's out of your hands." Justice was process, not outcome.

Taking cases forward was seen as not just a legal, but a moral, act. An officer described this attitude: "Once I make the decision to take a person to court, I try and not let it bother me what happens because I have absolutely no control over what the court does. I take the matter to court and for the most part I try not to let what happens get to me. If the person gets slapped on the wrist or the person gets found not guilty, I've done what I think legally and morally I have to do. You just can't let the court situation bother you." Regardless of the outcome, many officers felt that they had a moral duty to take certain respondents to court.

When cruelty or neglect was extreme, they often prosecuted even if cases were not likely to be received well in court. In one such instance, a respondent beat his dog to death with a hammer. The officer believed that it was mandatory to take this case to court, despite the respondent's contriteness, which could

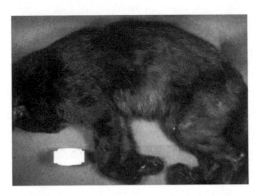

work against a guilty verdict. He said, "I will at least get it into court, whatever happens there. Just to do that . . . I know he was remorseful for it, but he did hit his dog at least ten times with the blunt end of the hammer and he was holding the dog by the collar. I have to do something about it." Sometimes officers were morally outraged because respondents received re-

Officers felt they had a moral duty to prosecute the respondent who shot this cat.

peated warnings over years, only to ignore these warnings—at the animal's expense. An officer described a case that moved him to take legal action, despite the adverse outcome he expected in court, because the respondent chronically neglected her horse over several years by not trimming its six-inch hooves. "That can be very painful to a horse. It can cause the tendons to be contracted, and basically the horse was walking like it had size twelve shoes on. And I went there with Officer Jill. The woman wasn't home. I left a card. The horse was on the ground. It was too painful for the horse to stand." He got in touch with her the next morning, giving her an option to surrender the horse or have it seized. Although she surrendered the horse, the officer filed charges against her. "I can't let that go. She was warned before. She was warned in '95 by Officer Jill for the same thing." The officer took this legal action, even though the woman had no record and he was almost certain not to get a guilty verdict "unless it's a real violent crime. Maybe continued without a finding, some sort of fine, which isn't much. At least she'll be brought up to the court, and continued without a finding is at least something. It will be a wake up call for her. She'll know that it is obviously a violation of law and won't be tolerated."

Although they prosecuted moral cases, officers still faced disappointing trial outcomes. Rookies looked for guilty verdicts, harsh fines, and even jail time in cruelty cases they took to court. Maintaining this expectation led to an almost constant sense of failure. With more experience, most officers developed a different definition of success in court that gave them a sense of accomplishment. They learned to redefine their concept of legal victory. For example, some spoke about how "good prosecutions made it all the better." One officer, for instance, described why he felt effective: "Anytime you get a complaint issued that goes through the court process and you get some kind of finding that puts this person on notice, I think it's a victory. When it's not a victory is when you get a not guilty. Anything short of a not guilty, as far as I am concerned, has some type of impact. Maybe it didn't have the impact you wanted. Maybe you wanted a guilty with a thousand dollar fine and got it, but the person was only fined $500. The person was still put on notice." Similarly, another officer said that getting something "on the record" was the most important goal when taking cases to court: "Okay, it's a year in jail, a thousand dollar fine, or both. You think they [respondents] are going to get one or the other. That's what most people think when you are new to this work. Now, what I want is some fine, probation perhaps—just so it's on record. And this will always be on a person's record—that this person was charged with animal cruelty—so somebody knows that this person did it before. They know that the law was applied in that case and the next time, it's going to be stricter." Even a ruling of "continued without a finding," which normally disappointed officers, could be viewed as a victory of sorts because "it really isn't dismissed. It stays on a person's record and any judge looking at it or DA looking at it considers it a possible conviction."

If going to court cost respondents time or money, this punishment was seen as a victory too. As one officer said of such a case, "Like I tried to explain to the owner of the cat, 'We've been in court three times. The first time we were here for four hours, the second time we were here for five hours, and today we were here for six hours.' He's paying that attorney 'X' amount of dollars an hour once he hits the courtroom. Plus he is paying him to do research. This is costing him some money." Another department member talked about how respondents were "punished." He noted, "Officer Fred had a case where he almost had enough to prosecute and it was like, it's not going to go anywhere. But you know what, take out the complaint just to make her miss a day of work, just to make her life miserable kind of thing. You sort of have to find ways to punish them, in a way."

Although they redefined what it meant to win in court, prosecution could still be disappointing. When this happened it "got to" officers, but they tried to be "realistic." In one drawn-out case, horses were found to have improper shelter and to be poorly fed, but the officer gave the respondents a "break" because they promised to improve these conditions. However, their barn soon burned down, so the officer gave the respondents six months to rebuild it, but they kept "giving me the runaround." So the department seized the horses and had them for four months until the respondents sued to regain the animals. The officer saw this as a "frivolous" lawsuit "basically to put up a smoke screen." "We ended up with this liberal, do-nothing judge that pretty much tapped them on the wrist and ordered us to give their horses back to them. I came home after that one and I said to my wife, 'I don't even know why I bother.' But you can't allow that to affect how you do the job because if you did, you'd never take anything to court. You have to be a realist. You have to look at it from a standpoint that it's important to you, but it may not be as important over the whole scope of things to some of the other people you're dealing with."

Being realistic meant that officers pursued a different strategy to be effective in court. Instead of focusing on the process of getting cases into court or redefining those outcomes, they tried to change the receptiveness of court officials to animal cruelty cases through education. Despite not seeing immediate gains with this approach, officers hoped to chip away at the court's lack of receptivity to animal concerns. Of course, not everyone needed to be educated. Officers discovered a few courtroom officials sympathetic to animal concerns. For example, one district attorney in the state strongly supported the prosecution of animal cruelty cases. An officer said of her, "She just does not like animal abusers. She puts time and effort into these cases. There are other DA's, but [with] pretty much all animal cases she has said, 'I'll handle them.' So she's the animal person." Similarly, one judge, known as an animal ally, gave hope to officers in one case. The respondent, who admitted to killing his dog, faced a possible guilty charge, a $1,000 fine, a requirement that no more pets be owned, and court-ordered counseling. Unlike many cases, however, the officer involved felt encouraged about the impending trial because the judge was an animal lover who had two Rottweilers. After rendering a guilty verdict and fine, the judge was overheard to say, "These are the worst cases."

Since only some courtroom officials were receptive, officers tried to humanely educate thee others. They believed that by continuing to take cases to court, officials would eventually regard animal cruelty with greater urgency and importance. As one officer said, "The courts will realize that animal cases are serious. We are bringing the cases more and more. 'Maybe we [court officials] should do something. Maybe we should become more familiar with animal cruelty cases.'" Such change occurred in one court, according to an officer: "In the Ashville court, they know me now. I go in, 'Hey, how ya doin'? You need a due date?' No problem. There is more awareness there. Maybe they will do something."

More than just exposing officials to cruelty cases, officers conveyed relevant information. One officer made a special effort to explain the anti-cruelty code to district attorneys because they were unaware of this law. When he had a case in court, he made an appointment with the assistant district attorney ahead of time to explain the law. Officers also tried to gain the support of officials by underscoring the seriousness of animal cruelty. One department member took photographs of harmed animals into court to show graphically what words could not. As he noted, "I have hundreds of photos. Some are collectors' animals. A lot of them are horses. Horses are tough to show when you go into court. A thin horse is a thin horse. It's hard to visualize." Officers' humane education involved more than relaying simple or straightforward information. Several spoke about "educating" key individuals in court so they could understand why certain incidents had to be regarded as animal cruelty. Officer Dan talked about how he disabused a district attorney's notion that it was acceptable to harm a cat because it walked in the respondent's garden. "He didn't have a clue. 'What's wrong?' he says, 'The cat was in the garden.' I said, 'It was wrong that the cat was in the garden, but the cat doesn't know he doesn't belong there. And there is no leash law for cats, so you can't use the leash law on them. Even if there was a leash law and a dog got out and the guy shot it in his yard, it still doesn't make it right. Just because he was off his leash doesn't give the guy the right to shoot him.'"

Officers believed that officials needed to be educated about the role of humane law enforcement, so they would be viewed as professionals rather than extremists. Part of building a good "reputation" was to show some deference to crimes against humans, thereby tipping their hat to the larger cultural view that animal crimes have less importance. One officer described this approach: "If you get to the court and you show the clerk that you've got an axe to grind and you're just taking people to court because you're kind of nutsy about animals, you don't get too far. If you go in there matter-of-factly and present it as, 'Gee, I'm just doing my job. I know this is not as important as the murder case or the rape case or something like that, but it is important in the scheme of things.'" Building a good reputation also meant convincing officials that everything possible had been done to resolve a case. This strategy was especially important when going to new courts and seeing clerks for the first time. As one officer explained, "When I go into a court that I have never been into, or see a clerk that I have never seen before, I gotta persuade him that I've done everything I could to resolve this, and I can't, and this is why I'm here." Once past this stage, clerks usually could be worked with.

Officers found ways to feel effective outside of court by focusing on aspects of their job where they could tangibly improve the welfare of animals. For one, experienced officers became confident that some of their actions helped to prevent abuse, even if they could not see this result. They believed that their presence at certain events had a chilling effect that stopped abusers from harming animals. One expressed this optimism about covering horse-pulling contests. "I think when we're there we're preventing cruelty, whereas if we weren't there, there'd be more cruelty." Another felt that his presence at livestock auctions had a definite effect on how well animals were treated, although he had to bear some taunting. He noted, "Just by being there they're being a little bit gentler with the livestock when they are pushing them through the auction block and things. They'll taunt you. The auctioneer will be up there doing his little chants. Then they'll hold up a rabbit and point at me and say, 'Oh, take me home.' They'll get me. They're not crazy about us being there, so they just kind of want to make fun of me."

The presence of an official at an ox pull will deter animal abuse.

Removing animals from bad situations was another extra-judicial way to feel effective. Even if cruelty officers failed to get a guilty verdict, saved animals represented victory. One officer noted, "If you don't necessarily get what you want for your prosecution, you might get a walk instead of a guilty. But if you get the animals out and back to good health and get them into good homes, that's what keeps me going." A colleague shared a similar view: "There are real routine days where you're just checking out complaints, and there's really not too much to them. You go home at the

Although the court case failed, officers seized this neglected dog from its abusive owner.

end of the day and you sit down and you ask yourself, 'What did I really accomplish today?' Well, you really didn't accomplish anything. But then another day, you might actually relieve a situation or get a search warrant and take some animals away from somebody and you feel good about that. You made a difference." An example of this occurred in a complaint against a couple who improperly housed and fed their cows. The wife had a restraining order against the husband because of domestic violence, but he was allowed to visit the property during certain hours to feed and water the cows. "The cows looked like shit. They were pretty skinny, shitty looking cows, and they were not being properly fed. We arranged for truckers to come in. It was an abusive situation. He was definitely taking advantage of her and trying to put the screws to her over the animals that were his, but yet he wouldn't provide any feed for them. And I just felt good that we were able to go in there one day and grab all them cows—get them out of there. They were sold to somebody else and it was basically a done deal."

On rare and very gratifying occasions, officers not only got animals out of bad situations but moved them to better ones. Reflecting on these unusual opportunities, an officer said that most cases that went to court were not "good because the animals suffered in some way if you ended up in court about it. You sort of concentrate on the cases that you got animals out of tough situations." To illustrate this technique, the officer described the following case: "I took this guy to court because he cut the ears and tail off a dog with a pair of scissors and the dog actually got adopted to a great family. Odd looking thing because it

"Beautiful Joe" might be funny-looking, but he found a wonderful new home.

doesn't have any ears or tail now, but somebody actually got involved and became a witness and came to court. Sometimes the outcome isn't always how you like it, but that dog could have had its ears and tail cut off and had a nasty life. But now it got out of there and it got a good home." At least one officer, in fact, checked to see if surrendered animals were adopted from shelters. As he said, "Sometimes they've been put down. Other times they have been adopted out and they are doing great. I think that's rewarding—to see an animal have a nice home."

It gratified officers to see even small improvements in the treatment of animals. Rather than trying to change the entire human-animal relationship between respondents and their charges, officers focused on improving specific behaviors, perhaps after repeated visits. One dealt with a respondent who had many behaviors that ideally could be bettered, but the humane officer took the following tactic to change a few:

> I didn't mention the chain because by law that chain is okay [officer wanted to see a longer chain on the dog, but did not advise it]. He's got normal posture movements, he can move around. If there wasn't all that junk around, he wouldn't be getting tangled [officer would like to have seen the backyard cleaned up, but did not advise it]. I want him to concentrate on stuff he's gotta change, but I'll have to do a recheck here. I have a feeling that that's what he was using, that barrel for shelter, which is better than nothing, but it's not going to cut it [officer suggests getting a dog house]. I think that dirty bucket, that's dirty little . . . I think that was supposed to be the dog's water [officer would

like to have seen a cleaner bowl of water, but did not advise it]. You can change what you can change. If the dog gets a dog house and you drive by and it's sitting in it when it's pouring rain, it makes your life a little better.

Another officer felt successful when he saw a respondent make small but important changes, including improving his dog's line to prevent tangling and provide better access to its doghouse. Speaking of this improvement, he said, "You know, maybe the animal's got a better circumstance. You've done something. It's always an accomplishment if you better how they live."

Officers sometimes had to make these changes themselves if they wanted to feel effective and improve the welfare of animals. Animal-inclined officers, in particular, felt responsible for the well-being of animals and went out of their way to help them, even though they technically completed their investigations. In this regard, they exceeded official job expectations and efforts taken by most police-oriented officers. Some of these efforts involved staying longer at work to help. For instance, after one officer finished his regular case work, he drove to a respondent's home to check on the condition of his dogs. The officer did this "drive by" because the dog's owner told him that someone had tried to cut the padlock on his pit bull's cage and asked if he could "swing by" because if the dog got out, "it would really hurt someone." This officer also carried with him spay/neuter certificates for respondents' animals to attack the problem of pet overpopulation. In another situation, an officer investigated a complaint of a seriously underfed dog, described as "withering" in the complaint. After talking with the respondents and seeing the animal in question, he concluded that the problem was not that the owners intended to harm the dog, but that they could not afford to buy it food. The officer claimed that his visit prompted them to consider giving away the dog. "I talked to them and said, 'Do you really feel that way or is it that right now you're in financial difficulty? Was the dog happy, healthy, and alive before you had this problem?' 'Yeah, we love our dog. We take care of him. We water him and blah, blah.' 'Fine, I will be by in the morning with a forty-pound bag of dog food. I can't bring you money, but I can bring you dog food.'" The officer spent two hours after work visiting a local shelter and got a free bag of dog food, which he then delivered to the respondent's home. At other times, they used their own money to help animals. In one case, an officer personally paid for what he construed as emergency rations for animals perceived in need to allow them to remain with their owner. As he remarked, "Yeah, if someone has a cat, I'll go and buy a box of cat food that will last them a couple days. It's a couple bucks and it's gonna save a cat's life." Sometimes, helping out in these situations meant extra labor by officers willing to get involved. One even built a doghouse to allow a healthy animal to remain in its home with its adoring thirteen-year-old owner, despite his mother's offer to surrender the dog. He recalled the situation:

> The kid loves the dog, there's no two ways about it. The mother told me to take him. The mother was, "Just take him." I was like, "Well, can we work on that? The kid loves the dog. He's not a trouble maker. He's not a gang member or anything like that. Let him keep his dog. I'll help out. I'll build the doghouse right now, and that will take care of the immediate problem of the dog being out in the rain and all that." Why take the dog, put it in a shelter where it runs the risk of being put to sleep? I don't want to sound like bringing an animal into a shelter is a death sentence, but it very well could be, and it could be a death sentence for another animal that it's taking its space. If there's no malicious or intentional abuse or neglect or cruelty, and it can be rectified, then that's my ultimate goal. [But that isn't in your job description, is it?] No, my job description doesn't matter to me at all. I don't even know what my job description is, other than to investigate animal cruelty.

In these cases, officers went out of their way to provide some form of temporary assistance that improved an animal's physical condition or living situation. Helping animals gave them something immediate and tangible to see, a welcome relief from the bulk of their casework, where trying to make respondents more humane was time-consuming and hard to confirm.

Finally, they could feel effective by helping respondents more than or instead of animals. Expanding their role required officers to become "problem solvers," more akin to social workers than police. As one said, "Sometimes I don't think of myself really so much as a law enforcement officer as I do a problem solver. It's not really that you're going to write everybody a ticket or take everybody to court you deal with, but you have to try and find a solution to their problem so you can do your job properly." This officer added, "You're the middleman. A lot of times they don't know what to do, so you have to come up with something. They're looking to you, so you have to try and find a solution and try and work it out for them."

One problem-solving role was for officers to improve an animal's condition or treatment, rather than seizing it, so that it could remain with respondents. Both animals and respondents remained in the home, but the quality of their lives would be bettered. For example, an old dog suffered from an untreated case of mange and severely untrimmed nails, but the respondent's infirmity prevented her from taking the dog to a veterinarian for treatment. According to the officer investigating the case, "That's just neglect. But she's [respondent] got problems herself. If you took her dog away from her, you could kill that woman. It would just drive her crazy. She does love the dog. But she has no way of getting it in [to a veterinarian]." The officer made repeated visits to develop rapport with the respondent's daughter, mobilizing her so she would take the dog to a veterinarian and the mother to a physician. When that failed, he arranged for an ambulance to take the dog for treatment and then have it returned to the respondent.

Sometimes their problem solving called for removing respondents from inhumane or dangerous situations with the help of various public service agencies. Animals would be seized and respondents relocated to safer settings. An officer recalled just such a situation. He confided, "I always just feel for the animals and I really don't care about the people, but I was really concerned for this woman." Because he worried about her welfare, the officer would sometimes make unannounced visits to her home. He remembered his final visit: "I showed up just to see how she was doing and to drop off about twenty pounds of cat food. The cats all just jumped on it. And she was walking in bare feet on fresh urine that was on the floor. All four burners were lit and I commented to her about the burners. 'Oh, I'm making dinner.' There was nothing on the stove. There was nothing but the trash that was usually out on the counter. She wasn't cooking. And I couldn't take it anymore for the woman." The officer then asked the building inspector to visit her home, who deemed it unfit for human habitation. Various state social and mental health services helped relocate the woman to a different setting. Commenting on such cases in general, the officer said, "If someone can't take care of themselves, much less their fifteen cats, then it's gotta become something more than me looking out for the animals."

On rare occasions, officers' problem solving might even extend to helping respondents adjust to their relocation. In one case, the respondent could not take care of herself. Her legs were severely swollen. It got to the point where the visiting nurses did not want to go to their trailer because of the smell and sight of fecal matter and other waste. It was obvious to the officer that she had underlying emotional problems, exacerbated by the loss of her 120 cats, so he organized a crisis team to deal with this complicated situation that included shelter workers, police, animal control workers, and a veterinarian. "You'd have to go in for ten or fifteen minutes, come out and clear your head, get some air and then go back in again." After the cats were seized, the Board of Health condemned the trailer, so the respondent could no longer live there. Officers helped her relocate to a new home. One noted, "I used to make deals with her. I'd bring her food, kind of buy my way into the apartment." The officer also gave her a color television to help her readjust to the new home. When the case went to court, the respondent praised the officer's kindness and generosity, a comment noticed by court officials. "The judge kind of looked at me. The clerk came up to me after and said, 'Did you really give her a color TV? We're going to have to give you a new name. I think we're going to call you the nicest law enforcement officer in the country.'"

Sometimes their problem solving extended beyond respondents and their animals to family members. Here, too, officers might have to mobilize different community services to intervene in domestic situations. For example, in one animal hoarder case, the officer was concerned not only about the welfare of the 38 cats in the home, but the psychological and physical well-being of the respondent's child. The officer pointed out, "The kid's not in a good environment. I tried to talk to her about the kid. I talked to the kid. The kid says he's embarrassed to bring anybody home from school because of all the cats. The kid is also flea bitten. How could you leave a twelve-year-old in that environment?" After talking failed to change the child's situation, the officer contacted children's services, briefed them on the case, and urged them to intervene. He made further visits specifically to monitor the welfare of the child, while also tending to the ongoing neglect of the cats.

Problem solving could even extend to respondents' neighbors and might be entirely unrelated to animal problems. But these also gave officers a sense of accomplishment when they could help. In one abandonment case, the officer arrived at the respondent's apartment but found no people or animals there. Two neighbors who lived on the floor below approached him and asked for help because they were worried about the safety of their building, given the respondent's absence. Since the apartment was empty and ignored, it invited unwanted trespassers to enter and pose a threat to residents of the building. The neighbors led the officer into the respondent's apartment to show him that windows could be opened from outside and that the front door hinges were broken, preventing it from being locked. They asked him to speak with the landlord about securing the respondent's apartment. The officer called the landlord and talked to her about this problem, thereby reassuring the concerned neighbors that something would be done to improve the situation. Weeks later the neighbors telephoned the officer to say that the apartment continued to be neglected and that vagrants were intermittently living in it. Speaking with the landlord convinced the officer that nothing would be done to help the neighbors, so he contacted local housing authorities, who promised to intervene.

In their police role, humane officers sometimes tried to prosecute cruelty by taking respondents to court. However, very few respondents ended up in court, and, when they did, most were not found guilty or punished. This experience in court could feel more like a degradation ceremony to officers than the pursuit of justice in an impartial forum. According to Garfinkel (1956), certain events shame people through the ritualized exercise of power, transforming their identities until they are looked upon as "lower" beings. Going to court to prosecute animal cruelty could be viewed as just such a ritual, reminding officers of the aspersions of official agencies or members of the community. Taking the occasional "strong" or "important" case before clerks, judges, and attorneys represented a judicial ritual wherein conflict was masked and largely ignored. Both court officials and officers alike behaved on these occasions as if they disagreed only about the legal details of a specific case and as if they all were members of a law enforcement community within which each had a legitimate role. There was an occasional snide remark about the victim being "just a dog" or the sarcastic comment about the "dog officer," but much more lurked beneath the surface. The underlying conflict, never overtly addressed in the courtroom, stemmed from different views of the moral worth of animals. Officers, including those with a police orientation, were advocating for animals in court. By prosecuting their cases, they were saying in so many words that animals merited protection under the law, that cruelty was unacceptable, and that abusers should be held accountable for their acts. This view was not shared by many, if not most, of those present in court. Far from being taken for granted, the moral worth of animals was contested but never quite articulated in court. Rather, the conflict was tacitly understood by the parties present. In that setting, the prosecution typically fell apart, whether at the hearing stage or with the final verdict. Humane officers attributed their failure to the fact that they were prosecuting crimes against animals rather than people. The typical outcome in court served as a stark reminder of the distinct inequality of humans and animals. The latter were simply less important, and those advocating for them, hard to take seriously.

In the face of this courtroom reality, it would have been very easy for officers to become cynical about the prospects of combating cruelty, but they learned to manage their judicial frustration and shaming. Doing so enabled them to continue prosecuting cases and to maintain a semblance of self-worth as law enforcement professionals, even though the results fell short of their rookie expectations and outsiders granted them little legitimacy. To manage these problems, first they suspended and then transformed the lay, or popular, definition of what constituted a courtroom success. By separating the process of prosecution from the outcome of hearings and deliberations over cruelty, the significance of taking respondents to court could overshadow its meager consequences. In certain respects, officers' jobs ended at the point of setting in motion the wheels of justice. However, they did more than this. They singled out certain cruelty cases as moral prosecutions because the abuse was so egregious and the abusers so wanton. Moral cases, from the perspective of officers, demanded prosecution regardless of the response of clerks and judges. At these times, going to court was seen as a duty rather than a matter of discretion. This view changed the meaning of courtroom failure because officers *had* to take cases forward. If they failed in court, it did not mean that prosecution was a bad idea or that they did a poor job at presenting the case to officials. Moreover, even if respondents were not found guilty or punished in a formal way, informally they paid a price in lost time and, perhaps, expense. In the eyes of officers, this counted as a victory, despite losing the conventional courtroom battle.

Second, officers rethought the purpose of prosecuting abusers. Simply getting respondents to court sent an important message, putting them on notice that some people regarded their treatment of animals as unacceptable and that future disregard of animals would not be tolerated. Going to court also made it possible for officers to again don the hat of humane educator. Clerks, attorneys, and judges could be persuaded that animal cruelty was indeed a serious problem worthy of their time and effort and that officers deserved respect as professional law enforcers.

Finally, they looked beyond their courtroom experience for other ways to improve the welfare of both animals and people. Correcting such problems, even those well beyond the scope of cruelty, gave them the sense that they could provide at least a provisional solution for most troubles they encountered, whether they involved animals or humans. Like regular police, they discovered that their competence extended to every kind of emergency (Bittner 1990) and that their self-worth came from generalizing their expertise and applying it to the problems of specific cases. Unlike regular police, however, their very steps to correct emergent problems of any nature jeopardized, once again, their identities as police officers. Already nebulous in the public's eye, the role of humane law enforcement only became that much fuzzier as officers helped respondents get out of jams or quieted neighborhood disputes over barking dogs, to name just a couple of the many interventions they made that have nothing to do with either traditional policing or animal cruelty.

Some would say that these adaptations are *merely* "lowered expectations," as though accomplishing this is an easy task. Others might add that lowered expectations are themselves an unfortunate sign of cynicism common throughout the modern work scene. Both charges minimize the significance of making this adjustment. It is neither a simple task nor necessarily one that reflects hopelessness. It is something that all groups do, as they redefine or narrow their horizons after newcomers lose their idealism. They, too, could be accused of just lowering their sights to cope with the harsh realities of work life. It is the way groups maintain their identities and prop up their self-worth, and animal police are no exception.

Conclusion

Humane Realism

A key question underlies much of *Brute Force*, namely, how do officers adapt to and overcome the cynicism that comes with the job? As rookies confront the real world after academy training, they are surprised, disappointed, and even shocked by how ineffective they feel as humane law enforcers. They find themselves frustrated with cases where cruelty is hard to determine, complainants and respondents who are considered untrustworthy, a public who is indifferent to them or does not share their perceptions, and a justice system that allows abusers to go unpunished or untried. In the process of carrying out these investigations, not only is cruelty's significance minimized, so are the identities of humane agents when seen as second-rate "wannabe" cops or closet animal "extremists." This tainted occupational image reduces their authority in the public's eye. Learning that the idealism of the academy does not reflect their real-world experiences, various forms of cynicism ensue, including a sense of distrust of the general public, rejection by regular police officers, and betrayal or letdown by the criminal justice system.

This cynicism is not unique to humane law enforcement officers. Regular police have a similar experience when facing the realities of their work (Graves 1996). Many have documented the despondency of police who witness misery and cruelty but can do little to prevent it (Bonifacio 1991). Although such cynicism appears to be more common in large urban police departments and among the lower ranks, especially among college-educated officers, it is a common phenomenon. Organizational psychologists claim that these feelings can be countered if police work itself provides feelings of achievement, responsibility, personal growth, and recognition to satisfy the worker's ego and self-actualization needs (e.g., Scanlon and Keys 1979). There is little evidence, however, that psychological interventions significantly reduce this cynicism over time. Other suggestions to counter this problem also do not appear to work, including "compassionate" or "inspirational" leadership, team building, and participatory management styles where workers share responsibility and have a say in the workplace policies and practices (e.g., Covey 1991). Regardless of the type of intervention, the degree of cynicism among officers tends to increase during their first few years of service, then decline slightly before finally leveling off (Neiderhoffer 1969; Regoli 1977).

A similar process of increasing then declining cynicism also occurs among humane law enforcement officers. The key factor that controls downwardly spiraling cynicism is the development of humane realism, an attitude akin to that developed by professional students at the end of their training. Studies of newcomers in a variety of occupations, including medicine (Becker et al. 1961) and law (Granfield 1986), have found a pattern of initial student idealism followed by cynicism and then the emergence of a more realistic attitude upon graduation. As graduation nears, students increasingly accept the fact that they cannot accomplish everything they hoped for as novices, but that by resetting their goals to more specific and accomplishable aims, they could still feel they were making important contributions. Something similar, although more elaborate, happens to humane officers that enables them to deal with initial disappointments and to make their jobs become palatable if not gratifying. They become humanely realistic.

To become humanely realistic, rookies must learn how to cope with and make sense out of all the ambiguity they encounter after leaving the academy. Indeed, the ambiguity that permeates every aspect of humane law enforcement could easily make most officers quite cynical if they fail to develop ways to understand and manage uncertainties permeating their work. Discovering new attitudes and practical knowledge on the job prevents this.

One kind of ambiguity is organizational. This occurs when staff members work in a setting that has inconsistent objectives and where employees expend varying amounts of attention and energy. Rookie officers face this organizational ambiguity when they encounter the sometimes conflicting styles of policing that characterize the department. As we saw, officers do not have the same job expectations. Although they all have a genuine interest in and concern for animal protection, some are more interested in the police component of humane law enforcement and others in the animal side of this work. In response, the department embraces a humanely realistic approach by allowing for alternative styles of law enforcement. Indeed, if the department required a single style of policing, it would alienate one group of officers or become a muddled middle unsatisfying to both groups. These styles are also useful because they counterbalance and keep in check the opposing orientations, thereby moderating the department.

For the most part, these styles rarely cause serious friction. Rather than being fought over on a day to day basis, the tension between officers becomes a familiar backdrop to the everyday operation of the department. They learn to live with this contradiction as part of their work culture, such that their differences complement each other more than create controversy. Indeed, suggestions of a divided or even contentious department exaggerate officers' views of their careers and approaches to cases. They are more alike than not in most respects. Those officers thought to be police-oriented still have genuine concern for the welfare of animals, while those regarded as animal-inclined still work hard to be good police officers. So regardless of their orientation, most believe they can do both policing and advocacy as they perform their everyday investigations, creating a joint sense of humane accomplishment.

Organizations expedite such accommodation. They reconcile diverse beliefs and multiple interpretations by developing "equifinal" meanings for the joint experiences of employees (Donnellon et al. 1986). Although these meanings are based on different interpretations, people can still feel as though they share a common language at work, enabling them to think and talk about common issues. Consensus and culture can then emerge from different experiences, values, and sense-making styles (Choo 1998). To do this, equifinal meanings must be based on broad or imprecise language. Such vagueness allows employees to maintain their own interpretations of an idea or action while believing that others understand their views and share their interpretations. By retaining a certain level of ambiguity, equifinal meanings provide the white space within which members can improvise while they reduce ambiguity enough so that organizations can act.

Equifinal meaning buttresses humane realism among officers by unifying their different approaches around a common theme. Some cling to their noble rookie goals, while others search for new objectives. In either case, officers need to pursue a broad and elevated concept that serves as a reference point for how they should think and feel about their work. Without such aim, officers could descend to humane pessimism or futility. "Humane sensitivity" fills this ideological void, or the notion that officers and dispatchers are particularly tuned into preventing cruelty and promoting animal welfare. Although the concept is part of the department's vocabulary, it is never carefully defined. Instead, department members speak about humane sensitivity as though everyone understands its meaning, when in fact few do except in a vague and general way. This ambiguity allows officers, in an informal and personal way, to explore the meaning of humane sensitivity and create definitions that make sense to them. They each think they know what it means. In so doing, officers feel they measure up to it, while at the same time judge colleagues to be deficient in it. Because the concept is so vague, opinions about its meaning do not translate into rigid rankings of officers into a hierarchy of humane sensitivity or lack thereof. Failure to specify its meaning avoids undue competition among officers for possessing such sensitivity; most if not all officers think they have it and rarely if ever is an officer directly criticized or held accountable for not having it. Attempts to concretize the concept would likely eliminate or diminish its current value and function.

A second kind of ambiguity is environmental. Those whose work involves the public must contend with how those outside the organization understand their objectives and mission. Sometimes the surrounding culture can be unclear about the processes of an organization. If so, the social context can be difficult to interpret or conflicted in its messages when it comes to the meaning and importance of carrying out core organizational tasks. Workers cannot ignore this confusion and are forced to make sense of what constitutes cruelty.

Despite the department's goal to improve the welfare of animals, the meaning of cruelty is unclear and shifting. Officers figure out what cruelty is as they interpret the code and apply it to their investigations. Although they enforce the same law, different conceptions of animal cruelty are crafted that vary from officer to officer and from case to case. Further complicating its meaning are complainants, respondents, police, and court officials who have other ideas about what qualifies as cruelty and other expectations for how it should be handled in modern American society.

Humane realism reduces environmental ambiguity by classifying cases worthy of cruelty investigation from the mass of calls made to the department. For the most part, their experience with cruelty is to see it trivialized, given how the public views animal abuse and animal cops. Rather than "fighting the good fight" against egregious cases of cruelty, animal cops are overwhelmed with ambiguous or marginal complaints that must be "stretched" to qualify as legally defined abuse. Far too common are bogus complaints of cruelty, such as barking dogs or "thin" pets, which are excuses to get neighbors or spouses into trouble. If officers regarded all or most complaints as proper for humane law enforcement investigation, it would dilute cruelty to the point of meaninglessness and blur boundaries between humane law enforcement and animal control. Through complaint compression officers define many complaints as improper to investigate, thereby reminding them that their true work involves more serious incidents of animal mistreatment. Although the remaining complaints deemed proper for humane law enforcement usually fall short of extreme cruelty, officers learn to view these lesser cases of abuse as cruelty, nonetheless. This working notion of cruelty differs from the novice's by being clearer and more realistic, given the kinds of complaints commonly made to the department. By carefully defining legitimate abuse, officers maintain a sense of themselves as humane law enforcers rather than animal control officers.

Humane realism also reduces environmental ambiguity by equipping rookies with the necessary skills to make sense of vague complaints and unpredictable respondents. Novice officers experience some cynicism and frustration when they find that complaints are not black and white, animals are hard to represent, and respondents are untruthful, difficult, threatening, and noncompliant. Yet their training in the academy does not equip them with the knowledge and strategies needed to manage such complaints and respondents. They have to acquire ways of representing animals and protecting themselves that accommodate the ambiguities and dangers they face. Officers become talented at reading animals to discover cruelty, skilled at reading respondents to uncover humane insensitivity, and accomplished at using "the knack" to gain their compliance. Although these skills are not always effective—sometimes they do not tell officers what they need to know or get respondents to follow their advice—they are far better than doing nothing for the well-being of animals and officers. Without these skills, officers would feel they had little control over their encounters with respondents.

Finally, humane realism reduces environmental ambiguity by enabling officers to feel successful, despite the mixed and confusing messages they get about their abilities to fight and prevent cruelty. In the face of frustrating respondents who do not follow their advice, novice officers wonder how they can make a dent in cruelty. They learn to think differently about how to interact with respondents, adopting an educational style that suits the realities of most cases rather than a prosecutorial style that would leave them feeling thwarted if not useless. In the face of disappointing courtroom experiences, novice officers wonder if they can do anything to stop abusers. With time these rookie concerns ease as officers get news ideas about what constitutes success in and out of court. They learn how to regard themselves as making a difference.

It would be wrong, however, to paint too sanguine a picture of humane realism's ability to lessen ambiguity and cynicism. It is a paradoxical adaptation. Built into humane realism are the seeds of the very problems that plague officers. In their efforts to manage these problems by becoming humanely realistic, officers end up reproducing and perhaps furthering them. Their steps to cope only dig them in deeper.

This paradoxical quality is shot through the work of animal police. Nowhere is this more evident than in the department's realistic approach to allowing alternative styles of humane law enforcement. These styles can be carried to extremes if officers become overly absorbed with the police or animal side of their work. Police-oriented officers occasionally go too far with their "only a job" perspective and become humanely under-sensitized, if not generally alienated from their work. Signs of this include an unwillingness to take the animals' perspective in complaints, a reluctance to intervene in cases, and a marked pessimism about accomplishing much with respondents. Animal-inclined officers occasionally go too far with their "mission" perspective and become humanely over-sensitized, if not "addicted" to their work (Schaef and Fassel 1988). Signs of this include rescue fantasies, commonly found among those who work with victimized populations when they feel overly responsible for their clients' safety and want to rescue them from their plight, a sense of irreplaceableness on the job, and a strong "we versus they" perspective with clients and the general public.

When extreme, alternative styles of work create a palpable tension among officers who sharply disagree with each other's approach to cruelty and worry that either the department's image or the animals it serves would be jeopardized. To some extent, this tension has larger significance than merely being an internecine squabble between conflicting workers. Their occasional backstabbing, gossip, or disrespect means more than just the jostling of people for ideological position. The conflict reproduces society's confusion about the meaning of cruelty and the importance of animals. In the end, this larger ambivalence is writ small in the contradictory identities of animal police. Especially when carried to extremes, they ironically develop styles of policing that resemble the disparaging ways the public sees them. They become the images that rookies decry—second-rate cops or animal extremists.

Even when not carried to extremes, most officers make other adaptations that further cloud their occupational identity rather than clarify it. For example, the marginality of many complaints and the absence of a mandate to enforce the cruelty code compel officers to back off from law enforcement. Hardly a brute force, they become little more than humane educators who try to make people into responsible pet owners. From the public's perspective, this adaptation to the ambiguity of cruelty and the uncertainty of officer's authority serves to perpetuate both. At these times, animal police may identify strongly with the abused victims they protect—neither is taken seriously.

If both are disregarded, then cruelty will be too. Paradoxically, efforts by officers to clarify the meaning and importance of cruelty muddle the public's understanding and appreciation of it. Officers have an uphill battle trying to convince respondents, as well as the general public, that many of their cases constitute inhumane behavior. Their work is very different from the efforts of animal rights groups that sensitize the public to think about cruelty in its blatant, institutional form by widely publicizing alleged cases of abuse in factory farms or biomedical research labs. These dramatic and sensational cases are "sexy," as some call them, because they crystallize the idea of cruelty—they are icons of abuse—and stir enormous emotional support. Officers, by comparison, mostly investigate unsexy cases. They are ambiguous or uncertain reports of everyday abuse and neglect that barely meet the law's vague criteria for cruelty, as opposed to the rare, flagrant cases that most agree are unacceptable if not despicable crimes. These unsexy cases, comprising the bulk of complaints investigated by officers, do not rouse the public's sympathies because they seem trivial if not debatable. Humane realism is an adaptation to this ambiguity, enabling officers to make the best of at least some cases that could easily fall through the cracks and never be treated as abuse or neglect. They make sense of these complaints by sorting out those considered worthy of investigation, even when most cases fall short of being "obvious" let alone egregious. While many are rejected as animal control problems or neighborhood disputes, others are treated by officers as violations of the cruelty code, such as the proverbial "no water, food, or shelter" complaint.

Because most respondents do not see the latter as a wrongdoing or crime, officers spend a lot of time and energy trying to convince them otherwise. Regular police, court officials, and everyday people sometimes share this dismissive view, even with cases of blatant abuse, prompting more education by officers to sensitize the public to a broader view of cruelty than now exists. However, their efforts are dilutive in that they work from the bottom up rather than the reverse. By focusing on neglect cases that hardly violate the cruelty code, officers must fight an uphill battle to change the public's mind about what is or is not abuse. While they work hard to get the public to take these cases more seriously, the public tends to regard even serious cases with mixed emotions or even indifference. If anything, officers' bottom up strategy is paradoxical because these cases reaffirm for some that cruelty is a frivolous notion. People may be polite enough to listen to officers, but patronizing does not mean a change in attitudes or behaviors toward animals. By comparison, animal rights groups take a trickle down approach to cruelty when they focus on dramatic abuses of "higher" animals that elicit enormous sympathy and support, in turn sensitizing many to be on the lookout for abuse elsewhere. There is no corresponding trickle up strategy for humane officers. Their cases are unlikely to serve as beacons that light up the ever broader terrain of cruelty.

In some respects, the work of humane law enforcement is a struggle over these contested meanings of cruelty. However, the department should not be regarded as a middleman in this struggle or as a referee of its correctness, but rather as a bellwether or trendsetter for giving coherence and importance to the meaning of cruelty. In the end, humane law enforcers do not merely enforce the anti-cruelty law for those whose lives bring them in contact with animals in harm's way, whether that involves complainants, respondents, regular police, or courtroom officials. They also define, validate, and give life to it. And this is the challenge of cruelty.

References

Alexander, Lloyd. 1963. *Fifty Years in the Doghouse: The Adventures of William Ryan, Special Agent No. 1 of the ASPCA*. New York: G.P. Putnam's Sons.

Alexander, Rudolph. 1995. "Recent Legal Trends in Child Sexual Abuse Cases: Direction for Child Protection Workers." *Child and Adolescent Social Work Journal* 12:229–240.

Alger, Janet, and Steven Alger. 1997. "Beyond Mead: Symbolic Interaction between Humans and Felines." *Society and Animals* 5:65–81.

———. 2003. *Cat Culture: The Social World of a Cat Shelter*. Philadelphia: Temple University Press.

Allen, Davina. 2000. "Doing Occupational Demarcation: The 'Boundary-Work' of Nurse Managers in a District General Hospital." *Journal of Contemporary Ethnography* 29:326–356.

Alter, Catherine. 1995. "Decision-Making Factors in Cases of Child Neglect." *Child Welfare* 64:99–111.

Antunes, George, and Eric Scott. 1981. "Calling the Cops: Police Telephone Operators and Citizen Calls for Service." *Journal of Criminal Justice* 9:165–179.

Archer, Leslie, and Dorothy Whitaker. 1992. "Decisions, Tasks and Uncertainties in Child Protection Work." *Journal of Social Work Practice* 6:63–75.

Arluke, Arnold. 1991. "Going into the Closet with Science: Information Control Among Animal Experimenters." *Journal of Contemporary Ethnography* 20:306–330.

———. 2002. "Animal Abuse as Dirty Play." *Symbolic Interaction* 25:405–430.

Arluke, Arnold, and Carter Luke. 1997. "Physical Cruelty toward Animals in Massachusetts, 1975–1996." *Society and Animals* 5:195–204.

Arluke, Arnold, and Clinton Sanders. 1996. *Regarding Animals*. Philadelphia: Temple University Press.

ASPCA. 1867. *Annual Meeting of the ASPCA*, New York. 2 May, p. 28.

———. 1883. *Annual Report*. New York.

Bayley, David, and Egon Bittner. 1984. "Learning the Skills of Policing." *Law and Contemporary Problems* 47:35–59.

Becker, Howard, and Blanche Geer. 1957. "Participant Observation and Interviewing: A Comparison." *Human Organization* 16:28–32.

Becker, Howard, Blanche Geer, Everett Hughes, and Anselm Strauss. 1961. *Boys in White: Student Culture in Medical School*. Chicago: University of Chicago Press.

Bittner, Egon. 1990. *Aspects of Police Work*. Boston: Northeastern University Press.

♦ **References**

Black, Donald. 1980. *The Manners and Customs of the Police*. New York: Academic Press.

Blumer, Herbert. 1969. *Symbolic Interactionism*. Englewood Cliffs, NJ: Prentice-Hall.

Bonifacio, Philip. 1991. *The Psychological Effects of Police Work: A Psychodynamic Approach*. New York: Plenum Press.

Boushel, Margaret, and Marie Lebacq. 1992. "Towards Empowerment in Child Protection Work." *Children and Society* 6:38–50.

Brooks, Laurie. 1993. "Police Discretionary Behavior: A Study of Style." In Dun-ham, Roger, and Alpert, Geoffrey (eds.), *Critical Issues in Policing: Contemporary Readings* (pp. 140–164). Prospect Heights, Ill: Waveland Press.

Bryant, Clifton, and William Snizek. 1976. "Practice Modes and Professional Role Playing Among Large and Small Animal Veterinarians." *Rural Sociology* 41:179–193.

Choo, Chun. 1998. *The Knowing Organization*. New York: Oxford University Press.

Covey, S. 1991. *Principle Centered Leadership*. New York: Simon & Schuster.

Cooper, Andrew. 1992. "Anxiety and Child Protection Work in Two National Systems." *Journal of Social Work Practice* 6:117–128.

Deutscher, Irwin. 1973. *What We Say/What We Do: Sentiments and Acts*. Glenview, IL: Scott, Foresman.

Donnellon, A. B. Gray, and M. Bougon. 1986. "Communication, Meaning, and Organized Action." *Administrative Science Quarterly* 31:43–55.

Drummond, Douglas. 1976. *Police Culture*. Beverly Hills, CA: Sage.

Fennessy, R. n.d. "Presentation of the Animal Victim, and Laws Pertaining to Abuse of Animals."

Flynn, Clifton. 1999. "Animal Abuse in Childhood and Later Support for Interpersonal Violence in Families." *Society and Animals* 7:161–172.

Frielich, Morris, Douglas Raybeck, and Joel Savishinsky. 1991. *Deviance*. Westport, CT: Greenwood Publishing Group.

Frommer, Stephanie, and Arnold Arluke. 1999. "Loving Them to Death: Blame-Displacing Strategies of Animal Shelter Workers and Surrenderers." *Society and Animals* 7:1–16.

Fryer, George, Jenny Poland, Donald Bross, and Richard Krugman. 1988. "The Child Protective Service Worker: A Profile of Needs, Attitudes, and Utilization of Professional Resources." *Child Abuse and Neglect* 12:481–490.

Fryer, George, and Thomas Miyoshi. 1989. "The Relationship of Child Protection Worker Attitudes to Attrition from the Field." *Child Abuse and Neglect* 13:345–350.

Galvin, John. 1998. "The Big Cheep." GQ, November, 340–344.

Garfinkel, Harold. 1956. "Conditions of Successful Degradation Ceremonies." *American Journal of Sociology* 61:420–424.

Gillespie, Dair, Ann Leffler, and Elinor Lerner. 1996. "Safe in Unsafe Places: Leisure, Passionate Avocations, and the Problematizing of Everyday Public Life," *Society and Animals* 4: 169–188.

Giovannoni, Jeanne. 1991. "Unsubstantiated Reports: Perspectives of Child Protection Workers." *Child and Youth Services* 15:51-62.

Goffman, Erving. 1963. *Stigma: Notes on the Management of Spoiled Identity*. Englewood Cliffs, NJ: Prentice Hall.

——. 1967. *Interaction Ritual: Essays on Face to Face Behavior*. New York: Doubleday Anchor.

Granfield, Robert. 1986. "Legal Education as Corporate Ideology: Student Adjustment to the Law School Experience." *Sociological Forum* 1:514-23.

Graves, W. 1996. "Police Cynicism: Causes and Cures." *FBI Law Enforcement Bulletin*. June, 16-20.

Groves, Julian. 1997. *Hearts and Minds: The Controversy over Laboratory Animals*. Philadelphia: Temple University Press.

Harper, Douglas. 1987. *Working Knowledge: Skill and Community in a Small Shop*. Berkeley: University of California Press.

Hebden, J. 1975. "Patterns of Work Identification." *Sociology of Work and Occupations* 2: 107-132.

Heinsler, Janet, Sherryl Kleinman, and Barbara Stenross. 1990. "Making Work Matter: Satisfied Detectives and Dissatisfied Campus Police." *Qualitative Sociology* 13: 235-250.

Herzog, Harold. 1993. "The Movement Is My Life: The Psychology of Animal Rights Activism." *Journal of Social Issues* 49:103-119.

Hewitt, John, and Randall Stokes. 1975. "Disclaimers." *American Sociological Review* 40: 1-11.

Hochschild, Arlie. 1983. *The Managed Heart*. Berkeley: University of California Press.

Horejsi, Charles, Cindy Garthwait, and Jim Rolando. 1994. "A Survey of Threats and Violence Directed against Child Protection Workers in a Rural State." *Child Welfare* 73:173-179.

Horowitz, Mark. 1998. "Social Worker Trauma: Building Resilience in Child Protection Social Workers." *Smith College Studies in Social Work* 68:363-377.

Hughes, Everett. 1964. "Good People and Dirty Work." In Becker, H. (ed.) *The Other Side* (pp. 23-26). New York: The Free Press.

——. 1972. "The Study of Occupations." In Bryant, Clifton (ed.). *The Social Dimensions of Work* (pp.106-120). Englewood Cliffs, NJ: Prentice-Hall.

Hughes, Everett. 1993. *The Sociological Eye*. New Brunswick, NJ: Transaction.

Irvine, Leslie. 2002. "Animal Problems/People Skills: Emotional and Interactional Strategies in Humane Education." *Society and Animals* 10:63-91.

——. 2004. *If You Tame Me: Animal Selves and the Intrinsic Value of Their Lives*. Philadelphia: Temple University Press.

Jasper, James, and Dorothy Nelkin, 1992, *The Animal Rights Crusade: The Growth of a Moral Protest*. New York: The Free Press.

Kassebaum, Gene, and David Chandler. 1992. "In the Shadow of Best Interest: Negotiating the Facts, Interests, and Interventions in Child Abuse Cases." *Sociological Practice* 10:49–66.

Kilroy, Walter. n.d. "What Is Cruelty to Animals? A Humane Law-Enforcement Perspective."

———. 1991. "Testimony to the Quebec Parliamentary Commission." 7 May.

Kleinman, Sherryl, Martha Copp, and Karla Henderson. 1997. "Qualitatively Different: Teaching Fieldwork to Graduate Students." *Journal of Contemporary Ethnography* 25:469–499.

Lorber, Judy. 1981. "Good Patients and Problem Patients: Conformity and Deviance in a General Hospital." In Conrad, P. and Kern, R. (eds.). *The Sociology of Health and Illness: Critical Perspectives* (pp. 395–404). New York: St. Martin's.

Loseke, D. 1992. *The Battered Woman and Shelters: The Social Construction of Wife Abuse.* Albany: State University of New York Press.

McBeath, Graham, and Stephen Webb. 1990–91. "Child Protection Language as Professional Ideology in Social Work." *Social Work and Social Sciences Review* 2:122–145.

Meehan, Albert. 1992. "'I Don't Prevent Crimes, I Prevent Calls: Policing as a Negotiated Order." *Symbolic Interaction* 15:455–480.

Mennerick, L. 1974. "Client Typologies: A Method for Coping with Conflict in the Service Worker-Client Relationship." *Sociology of Work and Occupations* 1:396–418.

Metz, Donald. 1981. *Running Hot: Structure and Stress in Ambulance Work.* Cambridge: Abt Books.

Morgan, G. 1981. "The Schismatic Metaphor and Its Implications for Organizational Analysis." *Organization Studies* 2:23–44.

Morrison, Tony. 1990. "The Emotional Effects of Child Protection Work on the Worker." *Practice* 4:253–271.

MSPCA. 1995. "Job Description: Law Enforcement Officer."

Munro, Eileen. 1996. "Avoidable and Unavoidable Mistakes in Child Protection Work." *British Journal of Social Work* 26:793–808.

Nibert, David. 2002. *Animal Rights, Human Rights: Entanglements of Oppression and Liberation,* Lanham, MD: Rowan and Littlefield.

Neiderhoffer, A. 1969. *Behind the Shield: The Police in Urban Society.* Garden City, NY: Doubleday Anchor.

Noske, Barbara. 1997. *Beyond Boundaries: Humans and Animals.* Montreal: Black Rose Books.

Oppenheim, Lesley. 1992. "The First Interview in Child Protection: Social Work Method and Process." *Children and Society* 6:132–150.

Palmer, C. Eddie. 1978. "Dog Catchers: A Descriptive Study." *Qualitative Sociology* 1:79–107.

Perin, Constance. 1988. *Belonging in America: Reading Between the Lines*. Madison, WI: The University of Wisconsin Press.

Petersilia, Joan, Allan Abrahamse, and James Q. Wilson, 1987. *Police Performance and Case Attrition*. R-3515-NIJ. The RAND Corporation.

Prus, Robert. 1987. "Generic Social Processes." *Journal of Contemporary Ethnography* 16:250-293.

——. 1997. *Subcultural Mosaics and Intersubjective Realities*. Albany: State University of New York Press

Phillips, Mary. 1994. "Proper Names and the Social Construction of Biography: The Negative Case of Laboratory Animals." *Qualitative Sociology* 17:119-142.

Regoli, R. 1977. *Policing in America*. Washington, DC: R. F. Publishing, Inc.

Rigakos, George. 1995. "Constructing the Symbolic Complainant: Police Subculture and the Nonenforcement of Protection Orders for Battered Women." *Violence and Victims*. 10: 227-247.

Sanders, Clinton. 1994. "Biting the Hand That Heals You: Encounters with Problematic Patients in a General Veterinary Practice." *Society and Animals* 2:47-66.

——. 1999. *Understanding Dogs: Living and Working with Canine Companions*. Philadelphia: Temple University Press.

Savitz, L. 1970. "The Dimensions of Police Loyalty." *American Behavioral Scientist* 13:693-704.

Scanlon, B., and J. Keys. 1979. *Management and Organizational Behavior*. New York: John Wiley & Sons.

Schaef, A., and D. Fassel. 1988. *The Addictive Organization*. NY: Harper & Row.

Scocca, Tom. 1997. "Animal Police." *Boston Phoenix*. 3-10 July.

Scott, Dorothy. 1998. "A Qualitative Study of Social Work Assessment in Cases of Alleged Child Abuse." *British Journal of Social Work* 28:73-88.

Scott, M. and Stanford Lyman. 1968. "Accounts." *American Sociological Review* 33:46-62.

Skolnick, Jerome. 1994. *Justice without Trial: Law Enforcement in Democratic Society* (third edition). New York: Macmillan.

Sperling, Susan. 1988. *Animal Liberators*. Berkeley: University of California Press.

Stokes, Randall, and John Hewitt. 1976. "Aligning Actions." *American Sociological Review* 41:838-349.

Swabe, Joanna. 1999. *Animals, Disease, and Human Society: Human-Animal Relations and the Rise of Veterinary Medicine*. New York: Routledge.

Thompson, William. 1983. "Hanging Tongues: A Sociological Encounter with the Assembly Line." *Qualitative Sociology* 6:215-237.

Trice, H., and J. Beyer. 1993. *The Cultures of Work Organizations*. Englewood Cliffs, NJ: Prentice Hall.

Van Maanen, John. 1975. "Police Socialization." *Administrative Science Quarterly* 20:207-22.

◆ References

Van Maanen, John. 1978. "The Asshole." In Manning, Peter and John Van Maanen (eds.) *Policing: A View from the Street* (pp. 221–238). Santa Monica, CA: Goodyear.

———. 1992. "Drinking Our Troubles Away: Managing Conflict in a British Police Agency." In Hidden Kolb, Doborah and Jean Martunek (eds.) *Conflict in Organizations: Uncovering Behind-the-Scenes Disputes* (pp. 32–62). Newbury Park, CA: Sage Publications.

Van Maanen, John, and S. Barley. 1984. "Occupational Communities: Culture and Control in Organizations." *Research in Organizational Behavior* 6:287–365.

Violanti, J. 1981. *Police Stress and Coping: An Organizational Analysis.* Unpublished doctoral dissertation, State University of New York at Buffalo.

Wilson, James. 1973. *Varieties of Police Behavior.* New York: Atheneum.

Wipper, Audrey. 2000. "The Partnership: The Horse-Rider Relationship in Eventing." *Symbolic Interaction* 23:47–70.

Index